SAGGISTICA 16

Spectacles of Themselves

Also by George Guida

The Sleeping Gulf: Poems (2015)
Pugilistic: Poems (2015)
Letters from Suburbia: A Novel (2013)
The Pope Stories and Other Tales of Troubled Times (2012)
The Pope Play (2009)
New York and Other Lovers: Poems (2008)
Low Italian: Poems (2007)
*The Peasant and the Pen: Men, Enterprise and the Recovery of
    Culture in Italian American Narrative* (2003)

Spectacles of Themselves

Essays in Italian American Popular Culture and Literature

George Guida

BORDIGHERA PRESS

Library of Congress Control Number: 2015937928

COVER PHOTO: E. Annie Singer

© 2015 by George Guida

All rights reserved. Parts of this book may be reprinted only by written permission from the author, and may not be reproduced for publication in book, magazine, or electronic media of any kind, except for purposes of literary reviews by critics.

Printed in the United States.

Published by
BORDIGHERA PRESS
John D. Calandra Italian American Institute
25 West 43rd Street, 17th Floor
New York, NY 10036

SAGGISTICA 16
ISBN 978-1-59954-090-0

Acknowledgements

My thanks to Anthony Tamburri for encouraging me to do this book, and to the Research Foundation of CUNY for funding my research through multiple PSC-CUNY Research Awards. Thanks to New York City College of Technology, for valuing my scholarship. Thanks too to Bruce Boyd Rayburn and the staff of the Hogan Jazz Archive at Tulane University, and to Annie Lanzillotto, for their generosity; to Joe Corcoran, producer of *Tony & Tina's Wedding*, for his time; to Mark Noonan, Editor Emeritus of *The Columbia Journal of American Studies*, for his interest; to Bob Viscusi, for his proof that *The Sopranos* was worth watching; to Anthony Valerio, for his example; to Denise Scannell, for all her encouragement and love; and to the many directors, performers, and writers whose work have inspired me. And thanks to Joanna Clapps Herman, Bill Herman, Nancy Caronia, Peter Covino, Fred Gardaphè, Paolo Giordano, Josephine Gattuso Hendin, Dawn Esposito, John Paul Russo, Maria Mazziotti Gillan, Edvige Giunta, Fred Misurella, Maria Terrone, Dennis Barone, Alan Gravano, Ed Maruggi, John Domini, Rachel Guido DeVries, Joey Nicoletti, Joanne DeTore and all the other members of the Italian American Studies Association, for being a true community of scholars, writers and artists, who nurture the study of Italian American culture and literature.

Earlier versions of most of these essays and reviews have appeared in journals, as follows:

"*Eye to Eye*, by Maria Terrone," *Bookslut* (January 2015).
"Mafia Movies: A Reading List," *The Journal of Italian Cinema and Media Studies* 1.1 (2012): 114-119.
"Only the Zen Know Brooklyn: The Poet/Parent Wisdom of Diane di Prima," *The Paterson Literary Review* 39 (2011-2012): 58-67.
"*Heart Murmur*, by Michael LaSorsa Steffen and *And This is What Happens Next*, by Marcus Rome," *VIA* 21.2 (Winter 2010): 90-92.
"*American Gothic, Take 2*, by Maria Terrone," *Rain Taxi, Online Edition* 15 (Spring 2010).

"Prospero's *Muccs*: The Meaning of Martin Scorsese's Italian American Dialect," *Italian Americana* 28.1 (Winter 2010): 5-17.

"*Books and Rough Business*, by Tullio Pironti," *Italian Americana* 28.2 (Winter 2010): 107-110.

"Ink in the Streets: Dana Gioia, the New Poetry Wars, and Italian American Poetry," *Italian Americana* 25.2 (Summer 2007): 222-227.

"Anthony Valerio's *The Little Sailor*: Quintessence of an *Oeuvre*," *VIA* 17.2 (2006): 138-140.

"*Lies to Live By*," *The Paterson Literary Review* 35 (2006): 294-297.

"The Future Without a Past: The Humanities in a Technological Society," *American Italian Historical Association Newsletter* 38.3 (Fall 2005): 27-30.

"Las Vegas Jubilee: Louis Prima's 1950s Stage Show as Multicultural Pageant," *The Journal of Popular Culture* 38.4 (May 2005): 678-697.

"Anthony Giardina's *Recent History: A Novel*," *Italian Americana* 21.1 (Winter 2003): 105.

"'Cunnilingus and Psychotherapy Brought Us to This': Mafia Comedy and Italian American Culture," *The Columbia Journal of American Studies* 5.1 (2002): 82-96.

"Novel *Paesans*: The Reconstruction of Italian American Male Identity in Robert Viscusi's *Astoria* and Anthony Valerio's *Conversation with Johnny*," *MELUS* 26.2 (Summer 2001): 95-107.

Review of Anthony Valerio's *Anita Garibaldi, A Biography*," *Italian American Review* 8.1 (Spring/Summer 2001): 208-212. Reprinted by permission of the John D. Calandra Italian American Institute, Queens College, City University of New York.

"Dennis Barone's *Separate Objects* and *Echoes*," *Italian Americana* 19.1 (Summer 2001): 243-244.

"A Little Song, A Little Dance, A Little Ziti Down Your Pants: *Tony and Tina's Wedding* and Italian American Stage Comedy," *Perspectives* 23 (2000/2001): 11-19.

"Anthony Valerio: The Metaphysics of Frank Sinatra" (profile) and "The Don and the Lover," *At Your Leisure* (September 1998): 23-24.

"Mary Bush's *Drowning*," *VIA* 6.2 (1995): 201-203.

For Denise and Bradley,

who still listen when I think I have something to say

Table of Contents

Preface: On Spectacle (xiii)

Las Vegas Jubilee: Louis Prima's 1950s Stage Act as Multicultural Pageant (3)

Prospero's Mooks: The Meaning of Martin Scorsese's Italian American Dialect (29)

"Cunnilingus and Psychotherapy Brought Us to This": Mafia Comedy as Italian American Cultural Expression (46)

Two Mafia Cinemas: A Review Essay (66)

A Little Song, a Little Dance, a Little Ziti Down Your Pants: *Tony and Tina's Wedding* and Italian American Stage Comedy (75)

Mario Soldati's Italian Americans (86)

Novel *Paesans*: The Reconstruction of Italian American Male Identity in Anthony Valerio's *Conversation with Johnny* and Robert Viscusi's *Astoria* (92)

Anthony Valerio: The Metaphysics of Frank Sinatra (111)

Anthony Valerio's *Anita Garibaldi, A Biography* (115)

Anthony Valerio's *The Little Sailor*: Quintessence of an *Oeuvre* (120)

Only the Zen Know Brooklyn: Diane di Prima's Parent/Poet Wisdom (125)

Ink in the Streets: Dana Gioia, the Four Types, and Italian American Poetry (138)

Maria Terrone's *Eye to Eye* (147)

Maria Terrone's *American Gothic, Take 2* (152)

Tullio Pironti's *Books and Rough Business* (155)

Michael LaSorsa Steffen's *Heart Murmur* and Marcus Rome's *And This is What Happens Next* (159)

Fred Misurella's *Lies to Live By: Stories* (163)

John Paul Russo's *The Future Without a Past: The Humanities in a Technological Society* (167)

Anthony Giardina's *Recent History: A Novel* (172)

Dennis Barone's *Echoes* and *Separate Objects* (174)

Mary Bucci Bush's *Drowning* (177)

Index of Names (181)

ABOUT THE AUTHOR (185)

Preface
On Spectacle

Orson Welles once remarked that Italy is a nation of actors. He was right, of course, insofar as Shakespeare was right. We are, all of us, merely players—making it up as we go, falling back on what we know, commenting on the performances we watch all around. Italian and Italian American life have been full of what Luigi Barzini calls "The Importance of Spectacle," of life as show, a show that "can be so engrossing that many people spend most their lives just looking at it." Like the grand opera, whose richest source is Italian culture, the show ends in tragedy. But along the way, comedy rules the day. Italians have seemingly always known this, how to look upon even the most serious events—social upheavals, religious strife, invasions, revolutions, wars—with amusement, with a knowledge that they too shall pass, and in their passing be as ludicrous as they are grand. This clear sight is a gift.

In his well-informed assessment of Italian life, *That Fine Italian Hand*, Paul Hofmann notes, "Most other people throughout the world do not reproach Italians for lacking seriousness but rather seem to envy them: Maybe one should imitate them, and not look too earnestly at life and its vicissitudes." Through the centuries the Italian folk have known how to keep things in perspective. Hofmann might have added that Americans especially should imitate Italians. America's national business, after all, is spectacle: its popular culture, its lavish display of abundance, its imperial war machine. We should understand our spectacle for what it is, a show, and not, as many of us have come to believe, a manifestation of our exceptional virtue and vision for the world. *Sic transit gloria mundi* could well be the anthem of transnational Italy. It should be America's too.

These essays, however, do not pretend to address America's defects in ways that explore their many roots and ramifications. Their author intends them only to show how the Italian and Italian American gift for spectacle and appreciation of spectacle have enriched American popular culture and literature; how they have in that way infiltrated the American psyche; and how, in doing so, they have allowed us to question our own sense of exemption from the human tragicomedy.

Spectacles of Themselves

LAS VEGAS JUBILEE
Louis Prima's 1950s Stage Act as Multicultural Pageant

for Uncle Danny, who loved Louis

In her day Keely Smith was an American Madonna. Part Irish, part English, part American Indian (the part she has always put to stage use), she personified stoic sexuality. Raven-haired, somewhere between tawny and fair—"at once nut brown and pixieish" (Kamp 351)—Smith was a hybrid goddess: both 1950s American ice queen and classical object of male devotion; ideal of feminine reserve and idol of seductive motherhood.[1]

Louis Prima was an Italian boy. And Italian boys, probably all boys, at some point approach their mothers with a combination of fear, respect, worship, and sexual desire. This was Prima's approach to Smith on the Las Vegas stage. While his goddess stood stock still, the "ethnic bad boy" (Cuthbert, "Primo" F7) leapt around, shuffled,

---

[1] According to David Kamp, when she met Prima, Smith was "a 17-year-old girl raised poor but with impeccable southern manners," for whom "working with the likes of Prima...was a rough education in salty talk and the ways of a tomcat." Kamp goes on to explain that "even now, after decades of Vegas life, Smith still can't abide cursing and sexual frankness" (373). Yet, as Kamp and other music historians note, it was she who boldly engineered a 1947 audition with Prima's band, and later had an extra-marital affair with Prima's friend, Frank Sinatra. And the tryst with Sinatra may not have been her only one. Nick Tosches quotes a story from Ovid Demaris's *The Last Mafioso: The Treacherous World of Jimmy Fratianno*, a story in which Prima walks in on Smith and a casino dealer having sex in a dressing room. With characteristic humor and fury, Prima sneaks up on the offender, licks his scrotum during the act, then punches him out. So Smith's prim, yet lascivious stage persona may be as much Smith's as Prima's invention (86).

pumped his fists in the air, danced to the wild music of his band, and occasionally blew his horn with all the enthusiasm if not the technique of his namesake and "hero" (Boulard, qtd in Spera E5), Louis Armstrong. Prima played the rambunctious child for his mother/lover Smith's approval, which came in the form of laughter, mock Italian gestures, and calls of "Oh, Luigi"—but only rarely, and then only briefly. Smith stood, literally, for American beauty, America—both white and Native—to be made, New World consummation devoutly to be wished, obtainable but always at a certain distance from the Italian (ethnic) American who, like Prima, still spoke the language of his people.[2]

In this musical mating ritual, the language of his people served Prima well. His inclusion and zesty inflection of Italian dialect (among other languages) in his songs reveals a "genius" (Butera, qtd. in *Louis*) for the use of music, comedy and the nightclub stage as means of bringing people together through multicultural spectacle. He often incorporated Italian dialect phrases into his scats--like the wonderful sequence in "Just a Gigolo/I Ain't Got Nobody": *"ludu, ludu"* ("fight, fight"), *"tale tale"* ("just like that"), *"gernishe, gernishe"* (corrupted Yiddish for "gladly, gladly") *"stasera è l'om"* ("tonight I'm the man"), and *"ova linda"* ("beautiful egg," meaning breast or woman). Prima understood that the Italian dialect words he was singing, combined with the African American hep cat vernacular he was speaking, laid over a solid tarantella shuffle-beat foundation, because they did not make literal sense to American audiences, would make these audiences laugh at their surprising presence, and, through the humor of cultural sign and cross-cultural identification, would draw them and Smith closer to him and his multiethnic band. As audiences laughed

---

[2] David Cuthbert too notes the combination of ethnic comedy and "sexy horseplay" as a key to the act's success ("Primo" F7).

and tapped their feet to the relentless rhythm, Prima was allowing them to participate more fully in the American multicultural pageant than they ever had in the days of derisive laughter at Vaudeville's ethnic buffoons.

In the Louisiana of Prima's youth, Italian Americans often found themselves pawns in a racist game. Sometimes viewed by Southern white society as not quite white (Dormon 15; Mangione and Morreale 201-203), they frequently worked and lived alongside African Americans, both on sugar cane plantations and in cities. By and large, they "ignored the calls to racial hatred" that would have helped bring them into the white fold (Boulard, "Blacks" 54). As a result, they sometimes suffered discrimination on the bases of skin color and real or perceived cultural differences from Anglo American and white Creole society, which caused many Italian Americans to "find common bonds with Black Louisianians" (Dormon 15). In this environment, the two groups could and did share similar cultural beliefs and practices, many of which involved musical performance.

From his Italian (Sicilian) American upbringing and early interaction with African American and other Italian American musicians, Prima learned to use humor and music as both powerful means of individual and collective ethnic expression, and as reliable sources of income (Boulard, *Just* 12-21). He had the examples of fellow New Orleans Italian Americans Jimmy Durante, Leon Prima, and Nick LaRocca (composer of "Tiger Rag," who claimed to have invented jazz and who was part of the first ever commercially recorded jazz ensemble, The Original Dixieland Jass Band} (Hintz 101). Prima was raised in a centrally located neighborhood then called Back of Town and now known as Tremè, adjacent to both Congo Square and the French Quarter, and near what had been the red-light district known as Storyville—with many African Americans, a lot of them musicians (Schiro). As a youth Prima learned "how to make runs on a trumpet" from Lee Collins, an African American trumpeter who played the New Orleans clubs throughout the 1920s and 1930s (Lewis). In addition to this formal training, Prima could not help but soak up the "hot music" being played by his brother Leon (a coronet player) and other locals, as well as its musical sources: saloon blues and ragtime, and Sicilian marching band music with its spectacle and driving 1-2, 1-2 rhythm (Hintz 101; Schiro): all performed in the streets and clubs of the Vieux Carré.

Prima biographer Garry Boulard quotes Ronald Morris's comparison of the ways in which Sicilian and African Americans performed their music.

> The Sicilian approach to their peasant music offers five strong similarities to black music, sociologically if not clearly musically." Morris points to casinos where both Blacks and Italians were in frequent attendance, Black and Italian "itinerant musicians," parades, brass bands, and funerals, which were popular events with both groups, and finally a shared vision of what music represented: "Sicilians were much like black people in seeing music as a highly personalized affair, a reflection of an individual's feelings, although born of a collective experience. ("Blacks, Italians" 55)

One need only watch Italian American saints' day processions and black Mardi Gras parades to witness the performance of pre-Christian (both Italian and African) musical ritual—often at the heart of Italian American and African American celebrations—in the context of a nominally Christian society. These performances embody the spirit of jubilee, a time of sanctioned revelry and misrule. Prima saw them, and when he first rose to stardom at New York's Famous Door in the mid-1930s, often began performances by yelling out, "Let's have a jubilee!" (Shaw 109).

Both Saint Joseph's Day and Mardi Gras have become annual occasions for parades of black Mardi Gras Indians (Sinclair, "St. Joseph"). From 1750 on, African American slaves and American Indian peddlers interacted at Congo Square and its environs, on grounds that had previously been sacred to local Indian tribes (Sakakeeny 10-11). In the late nineteenth century, the African Americans of New Orleans were confronting the white southern reaction to Reconstruction. Many African Americans, some of whom were part Indian, began forming Mardi Gras "tribes," expressing admiration of the Indians who had resisted European dominance, and enabling themselves to play a non-European part in their city's annual spectacles (Sinclair, "Mardi Gras"). Members of these tribes created elaborate Indian marching costumes, which demonstrated a difference from white Mardi Gras "krewes"—social clubs which, since 1857, have existed to stage Mardi Gras-season balls and the parade itself—(Davis; Tallant 13)—who during that period tended to dress as figures from Egyptian, Roman, and Greek mythology (Davis). Every year since, the tribe marchers, like the krewe marchers, have sought to encourage a "second line" of revelers from among the spectators, to fuel the celebration (Sinclair, "Mardi Gras"). In both tribe and krewe festivities—parades, formal competitions, and masked balls—the men who comprise these groups have performed for the women of sister societies, most of whom have played the roles of spectators to be impressed (Tallant 3-46, 185-197).

Throughout his childhood and musical apprenticeship, Prima experienced most of these Mardi Gras and Saint Joseph's Day traditions (Boulard, *Just* 4): the men making a musical spectacle; the women watching and occasionally joining in. During that time he also learned to use comedy by observing the clowning of Mardi Gras revelers and of musician/comedians like Johnny "Candy" Candido (leader of the short-lived Little Collegians, a group that included Prima on trumpet), who had played the brothels of Storyville and were then playing the French Quarter's night clubs. Since the closing of Storyville in 1917, the Quarter itself had become "a pesthole of prostitution" (Rose 170), as well as home to many of the Big Easy's hottest clubs.[3] Its music, humor, sexual energy, and multiethnic character were "in Prima's bloodstream" (Casso 7).

By the time he left New Orleans in 1934 (the year Guy Lombardo discovered him playing at the Club Shim Sham), Prima had developed a habit of publicly blurring the race line. He emulated, without caricaturing, Armstrong's playing and singing style. (According to once hometown acquaintance, the young Prima reportedly borrowed (and failed to return) early recordings of Satchmo, from friends in New Orleans (Schiro).) During the 1930s and 1940s, Prima played the Apollo Theater to delighted crowds who took him for mulatto (Kamp 370). He was even barred from playing a number of white clubs, whose owners suspected, as did African American audiences, that Prima was black (Berry 33; Friedwald 57; Kamp 370). On other occasions he posed for the cameras with African American musicians. One photograph, published in a 1939 issue of *Down Beat*, shows Prima playing his horn for Benny Carter, Roy Eldridge, and Coleman Hawkins (rep. in Boulard, *Just*).

Eventually, to most of America, Prima became white, or at least an "acceptable substitute" for accomplished and crowd-pleasing black

---

[3] Prima first played a club called The Whip in 1927 (Boulard, *Just* 14). Later he played clubs such as his brother Leon's 500 Club, on Bourbon Street, and the Club Shim Sham.

bandleaders and musicians "in a racially dense America" (Beyer, qtd. in Cuthbert, "Hail" 3), even playing a large role in the career of another musician who during the 1930s and 1940s benefited most from the general public's preference for white musical stars. Although Benny Goodman was a Jew from the slums of Chicago during a time when anti-Semitism was often socially acceptable, he was also the most popular bandleader of the day, and his signature song was Prima's "Sing, Sing, Sing." While deeply held prejudices against Jews, Italians, and others lingered into the mid-twentieth century, the public accepted "Sing, Sing, Sing" as, simply, American music.

On the heels of his early success at The Famous Door in New York, where his "showmanship and ebullience, his jive patter and good humor, drew the jewels-and-orchids set" (Shaw 109) and helped put swing on the map and 52nd Street on the swing map (Miester 57), Prima moved to Los Angeles to start his own club, the Hollywood Famous Door. His popularity there led to an uneven career in motion pictures, beginning with 1936's *Rhythm on the Range*. In his twenty-odd films, Prima often plays himself or the part of a musician. Playing multicultural (primarily African American) music, he was a European American man acting African American, but doing so naturally, reverently, not in the manner of Jolson or other minstrels. He was an Italian American lady-killer—"'When he shouted, 'Let's have a jubilee'... a lot of those sex starved dames would practically have an orgasm'" (Weiss, qtd. in Shaw 109)—speaking with a Southern accent and entertaining the audience with gusto and a Satchmo sound. His persona was alluring, but must also have been confusing to producers and directors, who relegated him to cameo roles. Hollywood never would present Prima as well as he presented himself (Spedale, Jr. 312).

As his movie career fizzled and the swing craze swept the nation, Prima moved away from the combo jazz that first brought him fame. He returned to New York, in 1936 wrote and published the swing classic, "Sing, Sing, Sing," and in 1940 formed a big band, The Glee-Bee Rhythm Orchestra (named for Prima's unique shuffle rhythm). His work with this outfit, while it prolonged his popularity, also damaged his reputation among fellow musicians and critics (Boulard, *Just* 60). In 1945 a reviewer in *Metronome* noted, "As a leader, Prima has always been a favorite of mine, which makes me sorry to see him sacrifice his musical abilities to become a great showman" (Hodges 25). A year earlier, the magazine's editor and leading jazz critic George Simon observed that Prima's "blowing has become secondary to his showing" (22). On the road throughout the early and mid-1940s, Prima and his orchestra enjoyed good success culminating in *Metronome's* naming him its 1946 Showman of the Year. Two years later, Prima met the goddess of his jubilee. By that time the consummate showman/impresario, Prima was about to begin the most culturally significant phase of his career.

After auditioning the 16 year-old Dorothy Keely on a Virginia Beach stage in 1948, Prima immediately decided she would be his band's new chanteuse, though her name wouldn't do. The stage name he chose for her, "Dottie Mae Smith," suggests that from the outset Prima sought to highlight her mainstream Americanness. But Keely insisted on keeping her Irish family name in some form. They compromised on "Keely Smith."

The next few years were difficult. Gigs grew harder to land, and eventually, reluctantly, Prima dismissed his big band and performed many times with just Smith and a house band (Kamp 373). By 1954, the swing era was all but over, and Prima's popularity, sustained for years by 1940s Italian American novelty songs like "Angelina," and "Please Don't Squeeza the Banana," was a memory. Recognizing he'd once again have to reinvent his career, the resourceful bandleader assembled a combo similar in size to the one that played The Famous Door. Through a friend he was able to book a two-week engagement in a small Las Vegas venue, the Casbar Lounge, the Sahara Hotel's after-hours nightclub. The Casbar featured a tiny stage with one microphone, one spotlight, and an extremely low ceiling, which drew audiences much closer to Prima, Smith, Sam Butera, and the Witnesses than they had been to Prima's big band at venues such as the Strand in New York or the Saenger in New Orleans (Boulard, *Just* 105-106). This new group played five shows a night, from midnight to 6:45 a. m (Smith), all-nighters like those Prima had played twenty-five years earlier at The Whip in New Orleans (Pope A4).

In 1954 Vegas was a land of show-biz opportunity. A rapidly growing city of 45,000, it was luring more and more tycoons, players, mobsters, and celebrities every day (Boulard, *Just* 12-103). At first Prima and the band drew mostly hard-core gamblers, but before long they were also attracting big shots like Howard Hughes, John F. Kennedy, Danny Thomas, Frank Sinatra, Dean Martin, Sammy Davis and the rest of the Rat Pack (107; "A Louis Prima History"; Kamp 374), creating a sensation. The Casbar gigs led to national radio, television, and film appearances, and set the standard for all future nightclub acts. Prima's and Smith's eight joint appearances on *The Ed Sullivan Show*, often extended sets, beginning in 1954, reflect the couple's popular appeal during the mid and late 1950s (Kaz).

The success of their act owes to Prima's entertainment savvy, foresight, insight into American culture, and lucky timing. By the early 1950s, Prima had long understood the mass appeal of several musical and theatrical elements: Armstrong-style "hot" music; scat singing, a language of suggestive sound; Italian dialect spoken to an English-speaking audience (also a language of suggestive sound); musical call and response (notably in songs like "There'll Be No Next Time"), which Prima had learned to appreciate by watching Mardi Gras celebrations and black church services, during which he witnessed "the excitement that was part of worship" (Segreto, qtd. in *Louis*); a vaudevillian combination of music and comedy in a continuous show; multiethnic spectacle in the manner of Mardi Gras; the spontaneity typical of street-corner "cutting sessions," games of improvisational insult common among African American musicians, whom Prima idolized in his youth (Boulard, *Just* 13); Southern Italian *opera buffa*, with its focus on the "antics of lovers and current events" (Nakamura 145); and *bel canto*, with its emphasis on the singer's "flagrant self-display" and "seduction by which the desire of the singer and the desire of the listener are joined" (Connolly and D'Acierno 419).

Prima also understood that a perceptive artist can successfully alter song lyrics to please an audience, since lyrics organically tend towards their audience's language over time (Bellosi and Savini 145); and since melody can express emotions, without the benefit of lyrical translation, as Italian opera has proven (Connolly and D'Acierno 397). He had done so in a series of hits in English "heavily interlaced with the [Italian] slang of his... roots" (Tosches, *Unsung* 84) and often drawing on the melodies of popular Italian songs and rhythms. Among these were "Oh, Marie," "Angelina," "Please No Squeeza da Banana," "Felicia No Capicia," and "Baciagaloop (Makes Love on the Stoop)." Novelty acts that followed, like Spike Jones and especially Nicola Paone—whose 1954 hit *"La Cafetiere"* extolled the virtues of the Neopolitan coffee pot—kept dialect and other sonorous non-English phrases in America's musical consciousness.

Having blended these elements with his own brand of showmanship, the frenetic front man was able to present an act that transformed the Vegas lounge into grand scale multiethnic cabaret, a format that many American entertainers would borrow.[4] Prima recognized that Americans living in the post-War era would appreciate not only his group's infectious African American and Italian American rhythms, but also their performances of ethnic perspective and humor, as well as inter-ethnic sexual innuendo, which Prima carefully choreographed (Kamp 374; Maione, in *Louis*).

Prima's Las Vegas show reflects the reality that ethnicity in the United States has always been, at bottom, a product of imagination and performance (Boulard, *Just* 113-114), especially since the advent of television, which has both created and impressed American culture on citizens of all ethnicities in all corners of the country. Because of television, a national fear of communism, and a desire to enjoy long-delayed prosperity, 1950s America was increasingly a society of compulsory domesticity and cultural homogeneity. Yet, thanks to America's growing involvement in global affairs and to the movement of various ethnic groups from city to suburb, American society was also becoming more internationalist and ethnically heterogeneous. As the following few decades would prove, Americans, more exposed to the world beyond America, more comfortable with consumerism, and, after the 1965 Hart-Cellar Immigration Reform Act, more obliged to deal with a variety of ethnic groups, were ever readier to consume performances of ethnicity that, while still comedies of linguistic and cultural difference, were better grounded in reality than the caricature

---

[4] Tosches, author of *Unsung Heroes of Rock and Roll*, claims, "In Vegas, [Prima] became an actual paragon...of what a Vegas performer should be," and "His role in the evolution and creation of rock and roll is vastly underestimated" (*Louis Prima: The Wildest!*).

of Vaudeville and its later radio incarnations such as Fred Allen's "Allen's Alley" sketches (Halberstam 181).⁵ Many Americans were now beginning to see ethnicity not so much as a problem, but as an interest, a new (or renewed) source of identity, or just a pleasant escape from a cultural mainstream that the government as well as the television and film industries were manufacturing and promoting.

These and other cultural forces had readied the market for Prima's new product.⁶ In the wake of World War II, long-held racial and ethnic prejudices were losing force. Italians were rapidly gaining mainstream acceptance (as both white and civilized), as they moved to the suburbs, relied more on formal unions and government institutions, and benefited from a 1933 film code banning the production of pictures that incited "bigotry or hatred among people of different races, religions or national origins," a law which drastically reduced the number of fearsome Italian gangsters appearing on screen and in the national consciousness (Guglielmo 14). At the same time, the Civil Rights Movement was taking shape. The African American community was beginning to challenge the status quo, and the American public and legal system were beginning to take notice and take measures to end segregation (Halberstam 413-428). In 1954, just

---

⁵ Ironically, two of the investors in the original Famous Door, which Prima opened, were members of the Ipana Troubadours on *The Fred Allen Show* (Shaw 106).

⁶ To Italian Americans, Prima was providing a slightly different product. Robert Connolly and Pellegrino D'Acierno point out that Prima's songs are "authentic Italian American texts," because they are "double-voiced, addressed at once to the Italian American listener privy to the obscenities coded in the dialect and the American listener who regards those expressions as 'greenhorn' folklore" (429). If a member of Prima's audience happened to be Italian American, he got more of the Italian dialect and most of the gestures, which made him even more a part of Prima's act, and vice-versa. As radio personality Ron Cannatella observes, if there were an Italian American Mount Rushmore, Prima's face would be on it (*Louis Prima: The Wildest!*). And it would be smirking and winking at Italian Americans, who could see and hear their obvious reflections in his face, language, and rhythms.

months before Prima, Smith, and The Witnesses opened at the Casbar Lounge, the Supreme Court handed down their decision in the case of *Brown vs. The Board of Education of Topeka, Kansas*. (Still, on the eve of his first Casbar engagement, Prima had to leave the club in order to sit with his old friend and colleague Cab Calloway [Boulard, *Just* 106]. The management could not risk violating Vegas's existing segregation laws.)

Prima's stage show assumed audience tolerance, and conveyed the idea that ethnicity may be experienced and deeply felt by anyone willing to open ears and heart. From this perspective ethnicity itself is an act, and therefore something at which we may, and should, often laugh. This concept of elective ethnicity might be best expressed in the refrain of "The Sheik of Araby," a song Prima may have chosen because it recalled the carnival kings of Mardi Gras krewes, who in the first half of the twentieth century published "radiograms" describing their krewes' imaginary travels in exotic lands. These radiograms contained the names of krewe members "disguised as Arabic names and titles, but all easily recognizable to most Orleanians" (Tallant 49). One radiogram from 1947 begins, "What a week we had here in Araby..." (49-50). On stage Prima calls, "I'm the Sheik of Araby," to which Smith and Witnesses reply, "With no Turban on." Like the kings of carnival, Prima is, he claims, whatever he imagines and presents himself to be.

Many of Prima's Vegas numbers were in fact spectacles of ethnicity. One such spectacle is a sequence of the dialect standards *'Zooma, Zooma!" ("C'e La Luna")* and "Oh, Marie" *("Oje, Marie")* performed on *The Ed Sullivan Show*. During *"Zooma, Zooma!"* Prima carries on a half-English, half-Italian scat conversation with the Witnesses' horn section, while Smith stands expressionless and still, removed from the action. "Skit-a-lee-beep...(bop)...*Zooma!*...(ba-dap)...Be-la-ba-ba...(ba-ba)" and so on goes the exchange. Prima interprets the original Italian

Spectacles of Themselves—15

song's conversation between mother and daughter as a call and response of musical lines, and lets the beat express its playful mood. He leaves off translating subject matter. (The Andrews Sisters had already done that in their popular, wartime, English-language version, "Oh, Ma-Ma.")

The beat carries the band into "Oh, Marie," which Prima sings almost entirely in Italian dialect. Dancing and clapping, he pours every ounce of energy into performing an Italian troubadour's song for the unflappable Smith, who stands by watching, impassive, like a Mardi Gras debutante. Such an *americana* is not easily won, so Prima enlists the help of his own krewe, his own tribe, the band. The persona of the song swears to his love, *"Sòna chitarra mia!"* ("My guitar plays for you!"), so Prima pleads with Butera to play *his* instrument, the saxophone. Butera steps forward for *"una nota,"* which he cannot deliver for laughing. Prima notices and quips, "What's the matter, Sam? You can't play in Italian?" Naturally, Butera, able in the end nearly to match Prima's bilingual scats, can, like the rest of the band, play in either language. Butera's jazz-inflected solo during their cover of *"Torna a Sorrento"* makes the Neopolitan classic not only American, but also avant-garde and broadly appealing (*Louis*). In Prima's quest for Smith's and the audience's approval, Butera is his closest *paesan*, a deft swing saxophonist and crack rhythm-and-blues arranger whom Prima recruited from New Orleans, with whom he can shrug shoulders or share a linguistic joke and a good lick or two. The rest of the Witnesses are the European and Hispanic American first line of a multicultural pageant. (Depending on whom you believe, either Prima named the band during the first performance when, while thanking them, he realized they hadn't yet been named (Kamp 374); or Butera did under the same circumstances (Shea 5); or Prima named them more deliberately, as a joking reference to the "the well-publicized involvement of Italo-Americans in both organized religion and organized crime" (Friedwald 58).) And as their applause for these numbers shows, Sullivan's audience could appreciate the band's performance for what it was, a joyful, humorous expression of romantic love and ethnicity set to American rhythms.

Prima's ethnic humor, while boisterous, is always celebratory, never derisive. When Smith sings "Porgy" to Prima, he parodies the ballad's sentiment. She warbles, "Life is empty since you been gone," and Prima, now downstage of her, calls back, "I'm here, I'm here!" What he might play with minstrelsy, Prima instead plays with wry humor. One of his band's most successful lounge numbers (judging from the recorded response of the Vegas audience), "Coolin'," a Prima original, recounts, in letter form, Prima's and Butera's exploits on a working trip to Israel. "A couple of cats from the Hot Club of Israel met us at the airport," Prima explains. "One kid was from a *schul*. He said, 'I just come from a cool *schul*.'" Butera then joins in, and a deadpan Prima tells the audience that during the trip they called each other "Samele" and "Labele," their Yiddish diminutive nicknames. At some point, they are taken to "a swingin' place out in the desert." The password to enter the place is *"braciol',"* the Italian dialect word for *"braciola,"* a beef or veal chop or cutlet rolled and stuffed. In fact, Prima continues, sharing a chuckle with Butera, "The place was full of *'deliziani','*" Italian delicacies. "They were servin' marinated pizza with gefilte fish on the top.... They gave us a couple jars of *ricuttu*, in case we got *agita* from the gefilte fish" (Prima). Here, as in "Just a Gigolo/I Ain't Got Nobody," Prima employs Italian dialect and Yiddish together, reflecting a career-long "predilection for all things Jewish" (Friedwald 57). But the entire exchange is not just a string of good-natured, logocentric ethnic jokes. It is also a celebration of Tel Aviv as a "swingin' place," of Italian and Jewish soul food, of ethnic language, and of American ethnicity—the Italian dialect Prima uses being more Italian American than Italian, and Yiddish being more (European) Jewish American than Israeli Jewish. The exotic location, the ethnic food and language, and the inclusion of these elements in a thoroughly (African and Italian) American musical composition have the effect of "taking middle American culture and setting it askew" (56), inextricably intertwining it with other cultures.

While Prima's and Butera's on-stage relationship allowed post-War audiences to see Italian American men at ethnic play, it was Prima's on-stage relationship with Smith, more than any other feature of the show, that tapped into the nation's incipient desire for the celebration of ethnicity and for greater sexual freedom (Halberstam 256). The consummate impresario, Prima orchestrated the banter and physical antagonism between himself and his wife, which was the heart of their act. After observing Smith during their first performances together, Prima decided to present her as an erotic yet stoic ingénue, while he would present himself as a lecherous, smitten older man comically desperate for her attention (Boulard, *Just* 91-92). In time Smith and Prima assumed the modified stage roles of contentious yet affectionate husband and wife. But whatever else they were, they were perfectly paired stage opposites. On stage Smith is a natural balladeer; Prima is a swinger who admires and defers to her solidity, her American whiteness, but who tries continually to win her over to rhythm and blues, race music (Halberstam 456-479). "Keely was the sweetener," remarks Nick Tosches. "[She] would come in and sing sweetly in English" (*Louis*). She would, that is, establish a mainstream, white-bread mood, which ethnic bad boy-as-older man Prima would disrupt with his amorous clowning, his ceaseless jiving, and his band's back beat. Then, finally, haltingly, Smith would return her husband's admiration and affection.

A *Sullivan Show* performance of "Just a Gigolo/I Ain't Got Nobody" shows Prima trying to break Smith down, and occasionally succeeding. Each of the original songs of the medley—the 1929 German ditty translated as "Just a Gigolo" and the 1916 lament "I Ain't Got Nobody"—is about a man who has spent his entire life playing the romantic fool. The persona of each song knows he is bound for loneliness, and in the original version of each is thoroughly melancholy. But thanks in large measure to Butera's brilliant arrangement, the Prima medley becomes a winsome invitation to the audience as well as Smith, to join in the carefree life of the bachelor. While a bass thumps the opening bars, Prima leans over to kiss his lady love, who, when she finally surrenders a peck, quickly returns to frowning and standing stock still, hands at her sides. Both then rub their noses (which have touched), Prima amused, Smith apparently disgusted. As the medley continues, Prima jumps in with the boys in the band, scat singing, playing, snapping his fingers, and prancing like an insane but benign bear. Every few minutes he dances his way to Smith's side and pleads for her attention, which she refuses to pay, causing him in turn to lower his hands, still his feet, and wipe the joy off his face, though only for a few brief seconds, until he can no longer resist the beat. Finally, during the song's last, furious chorus, Smith gives in, tenderly stroking Prima's doughy mug as he belts out the refrain, but then only for a few seconds before she retreats to her scowl and aloof pose (*Louis*).

During another appearance on *The Sullivan Show*, Prima scats his way into "I'm in the Mood for Love," in response to a typically stern look from Smith, who launches into a classic bit of inter-ethnic comedy. In mock anger, she performs an Indian whoop. She follows this with a gesture more familiar to Prima, a flick of the fingers outward from the chin, the *"va' a fa' napola"* ("go to hell") gesture, which

"The Chief," as Prima was often called, because of his supposed resemblance to an Indian chief (Cuthbert, "Hail" TV3), acknowledges with laughter.

The couple's sexual cutting sessions could be equally entertaining, and daring, as this exchange from a recorded 1959 show at the Desert Inn illustrates.

> *Smith*: (to audience) Doesn't he look like the Indian on the nickel... I wish he was the buffalo.
> *Prima*: Once she gets home, she's dead, believe me.
> *Smith*: That's the only way we can start even, believe me. (*On Stage*)

While Prima could never get away with such explicit innuendo on television, he could present himself and Smith sarcastically blessing each other with signs of the cross, as they did during another performance on *Sullivan* (*Louis*). Like Mardi Gras revelry, Prima's act was full of comedy that challenged sexual and cultural taboos in a Christian context.

Since Prima's act, though different each night, was always a coherent *opera buffa*, I would recommend that those interested in experiencing it themselves either listen to all available live-in-studio or live-on-stage albums of the era[7] or arrange to see footage of extended sets from television's early variety shows.[8] In the meantime, I offer the following description and analysis of a televised, nearly full-lenth

---

[7] These include the Capitol Records albums *The Wildest, The Call of the Wildest, The Wildest Show at Tahoe, Las Vegas Prima Style,* and the Jasmine Records album *On Stage.*

[8] No critic of Prima's era carefully analyzed an entire set, but footage of extended television appearances is available for viewing at The Museum of Television and Radio in New York City, the Historic Films Archive in East Hampton, New York, and other film archives.

Prima/Smith/Witnesses set, along with a few concluding remarks on the act's cultural significance.

Unfortunately, Prima turned down not only a regular spot on *The Milton Berle Show* for thirteen weeks in the fall of 1958, but also, around the same time, passed on a weekly Louis and Keely show. He feared that television producers would try to censor what *Time Magazine* had that year deemed a "doggedly vulgar show" (Boulard, *Just* 118-119). The following spring, however, Prima, Smith, and the band had their lengthiest television appearance, a full hour, on the 500th episode of *The Dinah Shore Chevy Show*. The show aired on April 5th, 1959, by which time Prima and Smith had reached the zenith of their popularity. *Dinah Shore, Sullivan* and other variety shows, with their combination of music and comedy, were ideal broadcast showcases. In a 1999 article for *Vanity Fair*, David Kamp, the only other critic who has written of the 1959 appearance, described the band at that time as a "machine," and Prima and Smith as "a mesmerizingly odd couple" by virtue of the maps of ethnicity on their faces (351). Shore introduced them this way: "They're knockin' 'em dead at the Sahara in Las Vegas. Of course, we couldn't bring all of you up there to see them, so we brought them down here to see you."

As always the band opens with a medley of "When You're Smilin'" and "The Sheik of Araby." Prima sings and mugs, while Smith looks bored. Meanwhile, Butera and the Witnesses wail and sing choruses. When Butera takes his solo, Prima claps his hands and jumps around his Venus. She glares. In the next number, "Up a Lazy River," Prima does his best Satchmo, scatting about Dinah Shore and Chevrolet along the way. Again, Prima plays for Smith. "Relax yourself," he cajoles, highlighting the comic difference between the ethnic hipster and the mainstream ice queen.

Spectacles of Themselves—21

After the band's patented final triple flourish, the music breaks. Prima then steps forward to address the studio and television audience. "Got a little song, ladies and gentlemen," he announces. "This is from our movie, 'Hey Boy, Hey Girl,' which is being now released." Never once does Prima look directly at the audience. When he isn't looking all around like a shy boy, he looks into the camera, addressing the people he would never reach at the Sahara. The bandleader then introduces Butera, who breaks into a soulful version of "Fever." Between notes, the sax man flashes a Cheshire smile, while Prima leads the band on a silly dance around the stage, until he runs into Smith, who frowns her reprimand. Eventually, Prima exhausts Butera, and continues to clown his way around Smith, again like a little boy, now a boy trying to suppress his laughter among grownups. The song's subject matter (the fever of lust), as well as the African American groove of the music and of Prima's stage persona here suggest the taboo interaction of black boy (despite Prima's chronological age) and white woman, this time without a tragic outcome like the 1955 murder of Emmett Till. Prima can get away with this performance, because he is, by virtue of his ethnicity, his skin color, and his music, both black and white: exotic and amusing to the mainstream audience, yet one of them and certainly, as a long-time celebrity, a national familiar. Prima's outfit—black jacket and white slacks—underscores his racial ambiguity. In the end, Smith, seemingly against her will, joins him in song.

"Fever" done and gone, Prima deferentially leads the object of his desire to the microphone. The spotlight first shines on Smith alone, as she sings "It's Magic." Then the lights come up on Prima and the Witnesses, who are now playing a slow, string-heavy arrangement, with all the reserve of a white big band. Having made a concession to their mainstream audience, and to Smith's considerable talent as a balladeer, the band launches into their idiomatic jump-swing rhythm. Smith follows her first solo tune with "It's Been a Long, Long Time," during which Prima dances a mock waltz (with himself) in the background and flails his arms wildly like a lunatic conductor.

The couple then come together at the mic, to sing "That Old Black Magic," which, they make clear in their mutual gaze, now has them in its spell. Their version is raucous, Butera's arrangement arguably the best ever. Even Smith clowns now, imitating Prima's antics. During the breakdown, a conga-driven Latin rhythm rises from the swing, sending the couple into a mad mambo. The song ends with their perfect harmony on the word "love" and with a hug. Here all cultural currents of the act coalesce. Smith's voice, so clear and crisp, blends with Prima's high rasp. The American Madonna takes the Italian American boy to her bosom, their conduit a combination of African American and Latin American rhythms.

Other segments of the episode demonstrate a conscious effort to present different cultures in harmony. After Smith and Shore, the two Southern belles, sing an Irish song, they have this conversation.

> *Smith*: "It was awful nice what you did singin' a song for all your Irish viewers."
> *Shore*: "Well, our job is to try and please everybody, you know." "
> *Smith*: "Oh, well, if that's the case, what have you done for the Indians lately?"
> *Shore*: "The Indians?"
> *Smith*: "My people."

At which point they sing a duet, "By the Shores of Kitchicoomee."⁹ Still later in the show, as José Ferrer dances with Smith, Prima pleads, "How about the Italians?" making several Italian gestures for "What's going on here?" Smith answers, "Go find your own girl, Charlie." In response, Prima performs a mock Tango. At the end of the hour, Prima, Smith, Shore, and Ferrer gather to sing a final song, the Chevrolet jingle of the time: "Drive your Chevrolet through the U. S. A. America's the greatest of all."

Whether on television or the Vegas stage, Prima's 1950s act performed, night after night, an ineluctable American truth: that music, particularly jazz and its humor-inflected offspring—rhythm and blues, rock and roll, and, later, hip-hop and reggae—provide the first and most consistent medium of cultural exchange. Prima's, Smith's and the Witnesses' synthesis of America's ethnic cultures set an example that countless other artists have followed. Sonny and Cher, another Italian American/American Indian duo, adapted the Prima/Smith shtick for the hippie and post-hippie generations. In songs such as "You Don't Mess Around with Jim," Jim Croce echoed Prima's musical jiving. Credence Clearwater Revival, a California band, reflected a growing national consciousness of New Orleans rhythm and blues that Prima and Butera helped raise. In the mid-1980s David Lee Roth simply copied Butera's arrangement of "Just a Gigolo/I Ain't Got Nobody" note for note, using the song's video to burnish his playboy image. Madonna, a much more ingenious pop star, is, like Prima, an Italian American who grew up with African American

---

⁹ Smith released, and in 1994 reissued, a solo album entitled "Cherokeely Swings." Smith's own long-running lounge act includes both Indian and Italian jokes. Like Prima's, they are never ethnic slurs. In fact, Smith's solo stage incarnation incorporates lots of Prima. She herself admits, "If it weren't for Louis Prima, there wouldn't be a Keely Smith" (Seiler E2).

music. In music videos for "Material Girl," "Like a Prayer," "Take a Bow," "Vogue," and other songs, she, in the spirit of both Prima and Smith, slips into and out of ethnic and sexual personae (Paglia 6-13) as if they were negligee.

A father of swing whose music continues to grace Hollywood soundtracks ("Big Night," "Swingers" and a host of Mafia comedies) and television commercials (for the Gap and General Motors Trucks), Prima figured like Comus—god of revelry and namesake of the first Mardi Gras krewe (Tallant 115)—in the swing revival of the 1990s. As a musician and showman, he has inspired hundreds of neo-swing outfits like Big Bad Voodoo Daddy, The Cherry Poppin' Daddies, The Brian Setzer Orchestra, and the Royal Crown Review. Setzer released a passable and popular cover of "Jump, Jive and Wail"; and in 1996 released a song entitled "Hey, Louis Prima," whose lyrics address the long-dead Prima as a hero: "Hey, Louis Prima/Man you make'em jump and shout / I got a 5 dollar bet on a 2 dollar bill / You're gonna show'em what it's all about."

Prima has also had an impact on less likely followers. Hip hop / punk bands such as The Red Hot Chili Peppers, and crossover rappers such as Eminem and Proyecto Uno follow Prima's example of experimentation and showmanship. And then there is Lupa (Frederick Paul Lupinacci), an obscure Rasta-sounding Italian American reggae singer, whose off-the-beat "Zooma, Zooma!" based on Prima's song, is a multicultural gem.

For all of these artists and others, Prima and his band demonstrated the cultural currency of popular entertainment built on blues-based music and the comedy of cross-cultural identification, gifting post-War America a lighthearted, public rehearsal of multiethnic community.

Works Cited

Bellosi, G. and M. Savini. *Letteratura dialettale e folklore orale in Italia, con profilo di storia linguistica.* Ravenna: Longo Editore, 1980.

Berry, Jason. "Just a Gig Aglow: A Hurricane of Sexual Energy." *New Orleans* (Jan. 1999): 32-33.

Boulard, Garry. "Blacks, Italians, and the Making of New Orleans Jazz." *The Journal of Ethnic Studies* 16.1 (1988): 53-66.

Brian Setzer Orchestra. *Guitar Slinger.* Interscope, 1996.

_____. *Just a Gigolo: The Life and Times of Louis Prima.* Lafayette, LA: U of Southwestern Louisiana P, 1989.

Casso, Evans J. "Louie Prima: The Heartbeat of New Orleans." *Italian American Digest* (Summer 1996): 7-8.

Connolly, Robert and Pellegrino D'Acierno. "Italian American Musical Culture and Its Contribution to American Music." *The Italian American Heritage.* Ed. Pellegrino D'Acierno. New York: Garland Publishing, 1999. 387-490.

Cuthbert, David. "Hail to the Chief." *New Orleans Times-Picayune* 15 May 1983: TV3.

_____. "PrimoPrima." *New Orleans Times-Picayune* 25 Jan. 2000: F1, F7.

Davis, Jim. "Mardi Gras History." 24 Sept. 1997. *East Jefferson Community Online.* 4 Aug. 2003
<http://www.eastjeffersonparish.com/culture/HISTORY/history.htm>

Dorman, James. "The Great Migration." *A Better Life: Italian Americans in South Louisiana.* Ed. Joel Gardner. New Orleans: Italian-American Federation of the Southeast, 1983. 14-18.

"Five Hundredth Episode." *The Dinah Shore Chevy Show.* The National Broadcasting Company. April 5th, 1959.

Friedwald, Will. "Louis Prima: He's So Delightfully Low." *Southern Music.* Spec. issue of *The Oxford American* (Spring 1997): 55-59.

Guglielmo, Thomas, "The Forgotten Enemy: Wartime Representations of Italians in American Popular Culture, 1941-1945." *Italian Americana* 18.1 (Winter 2000): 5-22.

Halberstam, David. *The Fifties.* New York: Villard Books, 1993.

Hintz, Martin. *Ethnic New Orleans: A Complete Guide to the Many Faces and Cultures of New Orleans.* Lincolnwood, IL: Passport Books, 1995.

Hodges, John. "Louis Prima: Cry, Clown, Cry." *Metronome* May 1945: 25.

Jazz. Dir. Ken Burns. Public Broadcasting Service Home Video, 2000.

Kamp, David. "They Made Vegas Swing." *Vanity Fair* Dec. 1999: 348-376.

Kaz, Ed. "King Louis: The Louis Prima Story." 1997. *Cool and Strange Music! Magazine.* 4. 2 Aug. 2003. <http://www.coolandstrange.com/prima/prima.html>

Krase, Jerome. "The American Myth(s) of Ethnicity." *Shades of Black and White: Conflict and Collaboration Between Two Communities: Selected Essays from the 30th Annual Conference of the American Italian Historical Association, Cleveland, Ohio, 13-15 November 1997.* Eds. Dan Ashyk, Fred L. Gardaphè and Anthony Julian Tamburri, 1999. 103-116.

Lewis, Father Al. Interview with Lars Edegran, Hans Lychou, and Richard B. Allen. Transcript. 21 Feb. 1972.

"A Louis Prima History Lesson." 2002 *JazzRockMusic.com.* 2 Aug. 2003 <http://www.jazzrockmusic.com/LifeHist.html>.

Louis Prima: The Wildest. Dir. Don McGlynn. Prod. Joe Lauro. Perf. Louis Prima, Keely Smith, and The Witnesses. Image Entertainment, 1999.

Mangione, Jerre and Ben Morreale. *La Stories: Five Centuries of the Italian American Experience.* New York: HarperCollins, 1992.

Miester, Mark. "Props for Prima: The Italian Satchmo." *Offbeat* Sept. 1998: 56-57.

Nakamura, Julia Volpelletto. "*Canzone Napolitane*: The Stories Behind the Songs." *Italian Americana* 15.2 (Summer 1997): 143-156.

Paglia, Camille. *Sex, Art, and American Culture.* New York: Vintage Books, 1992.

Pope, John. "N. O. Jazz Great Louis Prima is Dead at 67." *The States Item* 22 Aug. 1978: A4.

Prima, Louis and Keely Smith. *On Stage.* Jasmine Records, 1994.

Rose, Al. *Storyville, New Orleans.* Tuscaloosa, AL: U of Alabama P, 1974.

Sakakeeny, Matt. "Indian Rulers: Mardi Gras Indians and New Orleans Funk." *The Jazz Archivist* 16 (2002): 9-23.

Schiro, Luke. Interview with Richard B. Allen. Transcript. 5 Dec. 1967.

Seiler, Andy. "No Jive: Keely Smith's Still Jumpin'." *USA Today* 17 Mar. 2000, final ed.: E2.

Shaw, Arnold. *52nd St.: The Street of Jazz*. New York: Da Capo Press, 1977.

Shea, Scott. "Louis Prima." Liner Notes. *Louis Prima: Collectors Series*. By Louis Prima. Capitol Records, 1991.

Simon, George. "Louis Prima: Louis Lopes to a Rating of B Minus Musically, A Commercially." *Metronome* May 1944: 22.

Sinclair, John. "Mardi Gras Day in New Orleans: Running the Streets of the Crescent City." 1997. Ikoiko.Com. 4 August 2003 <http://www.satchmo.com/ikoiko/js9703c.html>.

_____. "St. Joseph Night in New Orleans: Out After Dark with the Wild Indians." 1997. Ikoiko.Com. 4 August 2003. <http://www.satchmo.com/ikoiko/js9703b.html>.

Smith, R. J. "Louis Prima and Keely Smith." Liner Notes. *The Artist Collection: Louis Prima and Keely Smith, with Sam Butera and the Witnesses*. By Louis Prima, Keely Smith, Sam Butera, and The Witnesses. Capitol Records/Ultra-Lounge Wild, Cool & Swingin' Series, 1999.

Spedale, Rhodes J., Jr. "Just a Gigolo." Book Review. *Louisiana History* 31 (Summer 1990): 311-312.

Spera, Keith. "Louis Lost and Found." *New Orleans Times-Picayune* 13 Oct. 2002: E4-E5.

Tallant, Robert. *Mardi Gras...As It Was*. Gretna, LA: Pelican Publishing, 1947.

Tosches, Nick. *Unsung Heroes of Rock 'n' Roll*. New York: Da Capo Press, 1999.

Prospero's Mooks
The Meaning of Martin Scorsese's Italian American Dialect

But this rough magic
I here abjure: and, when I have required
Some heavenly music—which even now I do—
To work mine end upon their senses, that
This airy charm is for, I'll break my staff,
Bury it certain fathoms in the earth,
And deeper than did ever plummet sound
I'll drown my book.

—*Prospero, from Shakespeare's "The Tempest" (V.i)*

In the 1960s Martin Scorsese left behind his childhood and cultural apprenticeship on a "tight little island" (Mangione and Morreale 129) within an island—Manhattan's Lower East Side Little Italy—to become a filmmaker. He was part of the Italian American exodus to American places and people for whom Italian American culture could be convincingly refashioned. From a distance, with his first feature, *Look Who's Knocking at My Door* (1967), Scorsese began to recreate his island and similar civilizations for this new audience. Four decades after that feature hit the screen, most Little Italies have attenuated to the point that they exist only as culturally reductive simulacra—simulacra that cannot match the ubiquity and cultural perspicuity of Scorsese's more thoughtfully reduced recreations.

With the keen eye and attuned ear of a participant-observer, Scorsese, in *Mean Streets* (1973), *Raging Bull* (1980) and *Goodfellas* (1990), documents the language, lives and customs of the Italian American urban working and criminal classes, among whom he was raised.[7] For better or worse, these classes have for decades provided America with most of its popular culture images of Italian Americans (De Stefano 3-16), "of which language is the inevitable mirror" (D'Acierno 592). Many of Scorsese's characters perpetuate stereotypes of violence and crude behavior. But if we may say that these characters are stereotypical, we may also say that they are not entirely so. They do not, for example, enact the "linguistic disfiguration" (592) of Italian American men, the way the characters of *The Sopranos* (1999-2007) clearly do. Unlike Bobby Bacalá and Paulie Walnuts, they are not prone to malapropisms and mispronunciations. Most of them are, rather, men who have been raised to share their candid thoughts on personal matters and business relations with only their small circles of culturally like-minded men (Casillo 70; Howard 196-197). When they speak on these subjects, and on some others, they most often speak in code. This code may include the simple substitution of one English word for another: an abstract word like "thing" for "murder," or a slang word like "whack" for "kill," as in *Goodfellas*; or it may include the use of toothpicks and cupped hands to frustrate FBI lip-readers, as in *Casino* (1994). But the most complex code that these characters employ is Italian American dialect—which Laurino describes as the "Italian-American lingua franca...bred from the regional dialects of southern Italy, gradually mixing with the vowel off-glides and staccato rhythms of English speech" (111)—this dialect in an English-language context. Their dialogue is the cinematic record of an important Italian American artist calling attention to Italian American

---

[7] Both Casillo and Gardaphé note the documentary quality of Scorsese's Italian American films (Casillo 143; Gardaphé 69). Scorsese himself claims, "*Mean Streets* was an attempt to put myself and my old friends on the screen, to show how we lived, what life was like in Little Italy. It was really an anthropological or a sociological tract" (Thompson and Christie 48).

dialect; to Italian American men's complex verbal expression; to their puzzlement by the mystery, power, and limitations of their own world view and language; and to the limitations of the director's own method of exploring these subjects.

To many Italian Americans, Scorsese's perpetuation of working-class and criminal stereotypes amounts to *infamia*, public disgrace. But Scorsese is not just making Wopsploitation movies. He is inventing the Italian American screen human (Bloom 1-17),[8] revealing to the public the ostensible savage's psychological complexity and high degree of civilization. Just as Casillo sees Scorsese's antiheros like Charlie Civello and Jake LaMotta trying continually to redeem themselves, I see Scorsese himself trying continually to redeem both the stereotypical characters he is using and his own use of these characters. The success or failure of their redemption derives from Scorsese's success or failure to portray Italian American men not just as "people of the body" (D'Acierno 592) but as speaking subjects who are, like Caliban, grappling with language as a powerful means of expression, and who are grappling with their own connection to traditional Italian cultures and behaviors.

The pool hall scene in *Mean Streets* reveals the stakes of the linguistic games that Scorsese's men play. In the middle of the scene, Charlie (Harvey Keitel), Johnny Boy (Robert DeNiro) and Jimmy (Lenny Scaletta) are waiting for Joey Catucci (George Memmoli) to get money from the register, to pay a debt he owes them. After a disagreement with Joey over the volume of the jukebox, Johnny Boy refers to Joey as "this asshole," which leads to the following exchange:

---

[8] As Bloom understands Shakespeare to have invented complex, self-conscious characters for the English stage, I understand Scorsese to have done the same for Italian American working-class and criminal characters for the screen. Both men's innovation lies in characters' attempts to verbalize their complex perceptions of their lives and their language.

JOEY
All right. We're not gonna pay. We're not payin' because this guy

(pointing to Jimmy)

is a fuckin' mook…and we don't pay mooks.

JIMMY
I'm a mook? What's a mook?

JOHNNY BOY
A mook?

(turning one way)

What's a mook?

(turning the other way)

What's a mook?

JOEY
You can't call me a mook.

JOEY
I can't?

(Joey punches Jimmy in the face. A brawl ensues.)

"Mook" (or *"mucc'"*) is most likely either a corruption of the Italian word for *mucca*, "milking cow," or *mucchio*, "pile of garbage."[9] Jim-

---

[9] Casillo believes the word derives from the Neopolitan dialect word for *"boca,"* or "mouth," a translation that makes better sense, although it appears also from the context that Joey is calling the relatively quiet and passive (like a "mucca," shortened to "mucc'," or cow) Jimmy, not the loud and obnoxious Johnny Boy, a "mook," a fact that renders Casillo's translation nonsensical.

my, the person to whom the money is supposed to be paid, is passive and lets the hothead Johnny Boy speak for the group. For failing to speak for himself, Jimmy loses Joey's respect and his offer to pay up. He acts like a mook. *Jimmy* and Johnny Boy are genuinely puzzled by the word "mook," and are having the beginnings of a conversation about its meaning and usage, when Joey, frustrated, angry and interested only in avoiding payment, loses patience for further negotiation over money or language, and ends the discussion with violence. The brawl he sets off does not, however, actually end the discussion. Back at Tony's bar, Johnny Boy continues to dwell on dialect. "I just wanna know what does 'mook' mean?" A question to which he receives no immediate answer, although an argument could be made that, however disrespectful, irresponsible and thus dishonorable Johnny Boy may be, Charlie, in his weak effort to help his cousin escape a bad end, also acts like a mook

In the three movies under discussion, Scorsese's characters use Italian American dialect words or phrases a total of thirty times: thirteen times in *Mean Streets*, seven times in *Raging Bull*, and ten times in *Goodfellas*. On a few other occasions, characters speak standard— or something resembling standard—Italian, which, unlike their Italian American dialect, is translated in subtitles. This naked dialect calls attention to itself, crying out for examination that the characters, who themselves only marginally understand its power, try to give it.[10]

Most obviously in these three films, dialect serves as a marker of ethnicity. On this level the presence of the words, not their literal meaning, matters most. In the scene of *Goodfellas* that introduces us to many of the film's minor characters, Frankie Carbone (Frank Sivero) speaks to the dolly-mounted camera standing in for Henry Hill

---

[10] Scorsese is in fact the first American director to make programmatic use of Italian American dialect.

and for the audience. *"Pre', che dic'? Como se va?"* he asks, meaning nothing more than, "Hey, what do you say? How's it going?" Other characters in the scene use English-language code, like Frankie The Wop, who announces, "I took care of that thing for ya." Carbone's questions, however, emphasize the *italianamericanitá* of the world we're about to enter. In the party scene from *Who's That Knocking at My Door?*, Rosie (Marisa Joffrey), a girl at the party, asks J. R. (Harvey Keitel), Joey (Lennard Kuras) and their friends to "say something in Italian." Joey blurts out, *"Murte di fam'"* ("dying of hunger," desperately opportunistic), marking the boys' ethnicity in Italian American dialect that makes little sense in its context, except as such a marker.

Even to audiences who understand them incompletely or not all, dialect words can reflect an Italian American character's otherwise ineffable emotional response to common situations. Charlie, Johnny Boy and other characters in *Mean Streets* throw around *"Madonn'!"* and *"Minchia!"* so often in these situations that anyone can catch their drift. In one early bar scene, the one in which Johnny Boy first speaks, we hear him tell Charlie, "We got these two beautiful girls out there. We're gonna get laid. *Madonn'!* I met these chicks in the Café Bizarre. *Madonn!"* Right away the viewer knows what Johnny Boy is about, what occupies his mind; and even if the viewer doesn't understand Italian, he or she probably does understand that Johnny Boy is using the Madonna's name to italicize his lust for other women. Later, when Johnny Boy is shooting from a building roof and bullets are flying, Charlie yells, *"Minchia!"* as he runs for cover. The same viewer doesn't need to know that the word literally means "prick" or "penis," because in this context, he or she can easily surmise that it means something close to "Shit!"

On another level, words like *"Madonn'"* and *"Minchia"* express ideas and feelings that characters of this ethnicity, class, era, and place are supposed to understand. As the camera invades the privacy of Johnny Boy's conversation with Charlie, about the women he's found, his *"Madonn'!"* tells Charlie that this is a godsend, that finding these women in the Café Bizarre guarantees that they are "real Bohemians" who will give the boys sex. Afterward, in the back room of the bar, Johnny Boy describes a fake police raid during which he lost his money because he became disoriented outside of his neighborhood. "What happens?" he says to Charlie, who is expecting an explanation. "I came out in the yard, I don't know this building. *Minchia!* I don't know nothing. It was like a box...." *"Minchia!"* here underscores Johnny Boy's disorientation, a condition Charlie presumably understands, since he, like Scorsese in his youth, rarely ventures off his island within an island (Casillo 4-5, 69-72).

Italian American dialect also helps Scorsese's characters mark the boundaries of their islands, their neighborhoods, their social worlds, especially the boundaries between those worlds and the worlds of groups against whom Italian Americans have defined their own codes of behavior and their own whiteness in American society (Guglielmo 4-5). The use of dialect warns these characters against too great an involvement with America's racial or religious pariahs—whom they call *"melinjans"* or *"mulagnans,"* "eggplants" (blacks) and *"mazza crist',"* "Christ-killers" (Jews). The two "real Bohemian" women whom Johnny Boy brings to Tony's bar are both Jewish. Because they are Jewish, he assumes they will have the kind of casual sex without love that Johnny Boy, Charlie and their friends assume a nice Italian American girl will not. Of another Jewish woman at the bar, Tony (David Proval) says, "She's in here every night with a different guy. You know how they are." When Charlie makes a date with Dianne (Jeannie Bell), the black go-go dancer at the bar, he gets as far as taking a cab into Greenwich Village, definitely outside the boundaries of his neighborhood and society, then stands her up as she waits on a corner. In voice-over he says, "That's all I need now is to get caught in the Village with a *melinjan'*." The use of voice-over and dialect allows him to reveal his in-group code of behavior to members of the out-group, without, in his dialogue and on-screen actions, violating the in-group code of secrecy. He reflects his society's racial boundaries to a larger American audience, but at one remove, in a way that makes him more sympathetic than another Italian American character, Pino Frangione (John Turturro), in Spike Lee's *Do The Right Thing* (1989), who says in dialogue, directly and to members of his in-group: "We should stay in our neighborhood, and the niggers should stay in theirs."

Scorsese's Italian American dialect is not only a language of boundaries but also a language of traditional behavioral codes and the reinforcement of these codes, of the "truths that can only be perceived and validated by those within" the culture (Lawton 33). Toward the end of *Mean Streets*, an argument between Charlie and Johnny Boy causes Teresa, Charlie's girlfriend and Johnny Boy's cousin, to have an epileptic fit on the staircase of her apartment building. Johnny Boy runs away, and Charlie panics, trying, but not knowing how, to help her. An older woman (Catherine Scorsese) interrupts them, yelling at both Johnny Boy and Charlie in what sounds like Sicilian dialect, ending her rant with the epithet, *"Disgraziate!... Disgraziate!"* which can refer either to the two young men as "miserable" for not helping Teresa or can refer to Teresa herself, who is "wretched" in her condition.[11]

---

[11] Casillo definitely mishears the older woman's dialogue here, which he identifies as *"Graziate!"*, a "bitter thank you" that "shows only annoyance while parodying the idea of grace" (207).

Earlier in the film, in flight from a scene of murder at Tony's bar, Michael (Richard Romanus), Charlie, Johnny Boy and two minor, gay characters are riding in Michael's car. When Johnny Boy starts to talk about the murder, Michael reminds Charlie, whom he sees as Johnny Boy's keeper, of the need for silence on such subjects, according to the neighborhood's modified American *omertà*, the code of reserve (especially among strangers), honor, chivalry and unofficial mutual aid governing the lives of both the mafiosi and the laboring classes of pre-modern southern Italy and of twentieth-century American Little Italies. "Ay, Chaluzz, *stata zi'*," Michael yells. One of the gay characters asks the other, "You know what *stata zi'* means, Sammy." Sammy (Ken Sinclair) replies, "Sounds like something dirty." Here is one of Scorsese's many meta-turns on dialect, an on-screen interrogation of its vocabulary and speculation on its perception, in this case by people outside the culture. In-group characters know that *stata zi'* means "shut up," and they know why Michael has said it. Out-group characters hear it as Prospero first heard Caliban's native tongue.

In both *Raging Bull* and *Goodfellas*, characters use Italian American dialect to remind other characters of the danger and loss of dignity that accompany breaking the traditional rules of sexual conduct. In *Raging Bull* Jake (Robert DeNiro) abstains from sex with his wife Vicki (Cathy Moriarty), because he is training for a fight. His abstinence causes her endless frustration. In response, she goes out to a club with Salvy (Frank Vincent), one of the local don's henchmen, and a few of his crew. Jake's brother Joey (Joe Pesci) spots them there and, having already heard his brother's paranoiac questioning of his wife's fidelity, confronts her. He tells her that once Jake wins the title, things will be normal and "You won't have to go fuckin' runnin' around like a *twatson'*." "*Twatson*" of course is a portmanteau word, an English root Italianized to reflect the Italianate code of behavior it

Spectacles of Themselves—37

reinforces, meaning literally "big twat," an extremely undesirable label, particularly for a married woman living in the 1940s Bronx Italian American world the film depicts. A wife must never cheat on her husband, especially, as Joey well understands, the wife of a man liable to brutalize her if he finds out, and especially in a society that would see his brutality as justified by circumstances. (Joey himself brutalizes Salvy and is forgiven by Tommy, the local don.) So Joey decides to adhere to the code of discretion, to keep from Jake the secret of Vicki's night out, and in the process to save everyone's dignity. This choice ultimately costs him years of estrangement from his brother, although in making it he does what he believes he has to do. According to the traditional culture in which "being made a *cornuto* [a cuckold] is absolutely the most damaging occurrence that can befall an Italian male" (D'Acierno 612), Joey's choices of expression and discretion make perfect sense. Jake's greatest fear is the fate of Alfio, the cuckold, who must kill the popinjay Turiddu, to avenge the latter's affront to his honor, in Verga's story *"Cavalleria Rusticana"* ("Rustic Chivalry"), the basis for the Mascagni opera and the intermezzo from that opera, which, as Casillo points out, is Jake's theme song in the movie (229).

Goodfellas presents a comic, "double-voiced" (D'Acierno 612) and expansive version of sexual code reinforcement, in the scene in which Tommy (Joe Pesci), Jimmy (Robert DeNiro) and Henry (Ray Liotta) stop at Tommy's mother's house in the middle of the night, to borrow a shovel for burying the gangster Billy Bats (Frank Vincent), whom they have just ostensibly killed and stuffed in the trunk of Henry's car. True to a stereotype that has a firm basis in reality, Tommy's mother (Catherine Scorsese) takes the opportunity to whip up a full meal, meatballs and all. As the men sit eating dinner, she asks Henry why he doesn't talk much. When he responds that he's "just listenin'," she tells a story that comments on a time when it would have been appropriate to speak in defense of honor.

> TOMMY'S MOTHER
> You remind me of when we were kids. The *camparis* used to visit one another. And there was this man, he would never talk. He would just sit there all night and not say word. So they says to him, "What's the matter, *compare?* Don't you talk? Don't you say anything?" He says, "What am I gonna say? That my wife two-times me?" So she says to him, "Shut up. You're always talking."

> (Everyone laughs.)

> TOMMY
> *Cornuto content'.*

> JIMMY
> What's that mean?

> TOMMY
> *Cornuto...* means he's content to be a jerk. He doesn't care who knows it. He's content.

Tommy mistranslates for the two men who were not raised speaking Italian American dialect. The man is not a contented "jerk," but rather a contented cuckold, something any man with dignity, living in a society in which maintaining one's *bella figura* (positive and dignified public image) is essential, cannot be. Just as Tommy has failed to live by the code of *compareggio* (the comradeship of his closed society) by killing a "made man," he fails to translate the Italian American language used to transmit his society's codes for quasi-outsiders who have an interest in following them. The story and the failed translation of dialect are subtly ironic and consequential, because it is Henry whose talk ultimately sends Jimmy and Paulie (Paul Sorvino), his *capo*, to jail for good. The mother's story implies then that those who don't speak when they should, like those who speak when they shouldn't, are, in matters of sex, as in all matters of honor, contemptible.

When Scorsese's characters suffer from violations of traditional codes of conduct, they often respond in Italian American dialect to their loss of *bella figura*. In *Raging Bull* Jake must throw a fight to a mediocre opponent, so that the local mafia can make money on the fight. This is the only way they will allow him a title shot in New York City. After the fight, Jake's dignity lies in ruins. He cries alone in his training room. Later, the fix leads to a district attorney's probe and to Jake's public humiliation. Back home he complains to his brother.

JAKE
(Smacking an open newspaper with the back of his hand)
Look how they make me look. Like a bum. Like a *mamalucc'*.

JOEY
Like a what?

JAKE
Like a *mammalucc'* of the year.

"*Mammalucc'*" in dialect means a "dope" or "idiot," deriving from the southern Italian word *mammalucco*, a centuries-old term meaning "a mercenary in the service of the Egyptian king." Clearly, Jake has chosen this word carefully. He is in fact attentive to language throughout the movie. When Joey later tells him that his jealousy for his wife is going to "kill" him, Jake asks, "What do you mean 'kill' me?" insisting that Joey's choice of words "means something." Here, Jake labels himself a *"mammalucc',"* having indeed made himself a mercenary for the mafia, and in the process suffered public humiliation. But Jake needs take no action beyond complaint, because the mafiosi themselves are only indirectly responsible for his humiliation, and because they do in fact (four years later) give him his shot at the title. Joey's response to Jake's use of *"mammalucc'"* hints at Jake's initial failure to understand that he must compromise, abide by the rules of their society, to get ahead; as it hints at the brothers' joint failure to understand that the code of mutual aid has, at least in part, failed them. We see here too Scorsese's own awareness of the power and frustration of speaking a language that signifies in-group membership, but that also limits one's horizons and understanding of the world beyond that group's island.

In *Goodfellas* Carbone also suffers public humiliation. He himself breaks the code of reserve by buying his wife a "ten thousand-dollar mink," against Jimmy's instructions, in the wake of a huge heist their crew has pulled off. At a bar, in front of all their friends and associates, Jimmy tells Carbone's wife to "take it off," and, shoving the balled up coat into Carbone's arms, commands him to "take it back where you got it." As he walks away, Carbone complains only to his wife, *"Sta rumpiendome i cuglioni,"* in dialect that echoes the movie's most frequently used figure of speech, variations on "breaking" or "busting" "balls." He will not dispute Jimmy in public, because he is, throughout his screen life, a loyal soldier, and as such a true-blood, the most frequent speaker of Italian American dialect in the movie. He will not even take the liberty of using the English expression ("breaking my balls" or "busting my balls") that other characters freely employ. Instead, he muffles his displeasure in mink, the material of his own transgression, and cloaks it in mumbled dialect, a language only those inside his circle of Italian American criminals and dialect speakers (which does not include Jimmy) can fully understand. Carbone makes just this one mistake, but for it—like Johnny Roastbeef (John Williams), who buys a new Cadillac for his new wife after the heist, and whom Jimmy humiliates in front of her, chiding him, "What did I tell you?"—he dies at Jimmy's hands, a fact that effectively absolves him of the need to reclaim his honor by either "making a beef" with the bosses or by attacking Jimmy. Scorsese's camera lingers on the gruesome aftermath of Jimmy's massacre. The filmmaker here is no redeemer, even if the character he seeks to humanize could ever be redeemed.

In the end Scorsese, the sound of whose name itself recalls the word "sorcerer," should be seen as a kind of Prospero, who uses Italian American dialect and other deep cultural knowledge to recreate tight little islands like his bygone neighborhood. The director brings these societies to life, distorts them, exploits them, and only in part redeems their members. His cinema, like Prospero's magic, has brought Scorsese great power, but cost him cultural credibility, just as Prospero's art costs him "spiritual authority" (Bloom 667). He has sought to present a version of authentic Italian American life, but to find an audience for this presentation, he has highlighted the most dangerous elements of life and of individual characters on cultural islands that themselves have, in part and at least since his boyhood, existed as reductive simulacra. His characters' expression to an English-speaking audience is both energized and limited by its inclusion of Italian American dialect. Their worlds, like Caliban's, are little fiefdoms bound by medieval codes they must obey, though they neither fully comprehend, nor fully accept them; codes enforced and reinforced through a language that they both understand and do not, a language whose use renders them both stereotypical and human.

Scorsese's dilemma is, in essence, that of his characters. Language for all of them is both a cover and a light, concealing as much as it reveals about individual Italian American characters' complexity and their ability to express the complexity both of their minds and souls and of their societies. Scorsese's greatest fame, like Jake LaMotta's, derives from his performance of Italian American working-class and criminal brutality. Although Jake learns to recite, he is still best known for violence. He fascinates, because, like Caliban, he threatens the established order, and like Prospero, imposes a cruel order—and so repels us. Scorsese's projection of Italian American society and use of Italian American language reflect his ambivalence toward his native culture and toward the responsibilities of the ethnically conscious artist.

As Jake says in the monologue that opens and closes *Raging Bull*: "The thing ain't the ring. It's the play. So give me a ring where this bull here can rage, and though I can fight, I'd much rather recite. That's entertainment." His life of brutality and pursuit of redemption is finally rounded by a somnolent ex-pug's bathetic performance of language—from Paddy Chayevsky, Rod Serling, Tennesee Williams, and Shakespeare—originally intended to challenge and enlighten. His screen master has granted him language enough for us to feel his pain and see both his inferiority and the master's perversity. He and the other characters of Scorsese's Italian American movies are such ethnic stuff as dreams and nightmares are made on.

WORKS CITED

Barzini, Luigi. *The Italians: A Full-Length Portrait Featuring Their Manners and Morals*. New York: Atheneum, 1964.

Bloom, Harold. *Shakespeare: The Invention of the Human.* New York: Riverhead Books, 1998.

Casillo, Robert. *Gangster Priest: The Italian American Cinema of Martin Scorsese.* Toronto: U of Toronto Press, 2006.

Casino. Dir. Martin Scorsese. Perf. Robert De Niro, Joe Pesci, Sharon Stone. Universal Pictures, 1995.

D'Acierno, Pellegrino. "Cinema Paradiso: The Italian American Presence in American Cinema." *The Italian American Heritage.* Ed. Pellegrino D'Acierno. New York: Garland Publishing, 1999: 563-690.

De Stefano, George. *An Offer We Can't Refuse: The Mafia in the Mind of America.* New York: Faber and Faber, 2006.

Do The Right Thing. Dir. Spike Lee. Perf. Spike Lee, Danny Aiello, John Turturro, Ossie Davis, Ruby Dee. Universal, 1989.

Gardaphé, Fred L. *From Wiseguys to Wise Men: The Gangster and Italian American Masculinities.* New York: Routledge, 2006.

Goodfellas. Dir. Martin Scorsese. Perf. Robert De Niro, Joe Pesci, Ray Liotta. Warner Brothers, 1990.

Guglielmo, Jennifer. "Introduction: White Lies, Dark Truths." *Are Italians White?: How Race is Made in America.* Eds. Jennifer Guglielmo and Salvatore Salerno. New York: Routledge, 2003: 1-14.

Howard, Douglas L. "'Soprano-Speak': Language and Silence in HBO's The Sopranos." *This Thing of Ours: Investigating* The Sopranos. Ed. David Lavery. New York: Columbia UP/Wallflower Press, 2002: 195-202.

"Jimmy the Gent." *Crime Library: Criminal Minds and Methods* 2007. 20 Nov. 2007. <http://www.crimelibrary.com/gangsters_outlaws/gang/heist/3.html>.

Laurino, Maria. *Were You Always an Italian?*: Ancestors and Other Icons in Italian America. New York: W. W. Norton and Co., 2000.

Lawton, Ben. "What is ItalianAmerican Cinema?" *Voices in Italian Americana* 6.1 (1995): 27-51.

Look Who's Knocking at My Door. Dir. Martin Scorsese. Perf. Harvey Keitel, Zina Bethune. Prof. Joseph Weill, Betzi Manoogian, Haig Manoogian, 1967.

Mangione, Jerre and Ben Morreale. *La Storia: Five Centuries of the Italian American Experience.* New York: HarperCollins, 1992.

Mean Streets. Dir. Martin Scorsese. Perf. Harvey Keitel, Robert De Niro, Richard Romanus, Amy Robinson. Warner Brothers, 1973.

Raging Bull. Dir. Martin Scorsese. Perf. Robert De Niro, Cathy Moriarty, Joe Pesci. United Artists, 1980.

Shakespeare, William. "The Tempest." *The Complete Works of William Shakespeare.* New York: Avenel Books, 1975: 1-22.

Thompson, David and Ian Christie, eds. *Scorsese on Scorsese.* 1989. London: Faber and Faber, 1996.

"CUNNILINGUS AND PSYCHOTHERAPY BROUGHT US TO THIS"
Mafia Comedy as Italian American Cultural Expression

> *"These positive developments [in Italian American film] are accompanied by what might be called an 'involution,' an adherence to the status quo in that a good part of the production of Italian American filmmakers, minor as well as major, remains fixated on the gangster/crime film, which continues to serve as the primary vehicle with which to represent Italianness in mainstream commercial cinema."*
>
> —Pellegrino D'Acierno, "Cinema Paradiso: The Italian American Presence in American Cinema"

FADE INTO POSTMODERN CINEMA
       INT. A SOCIAL CLUB-EVENING

The interior of the club in Manhattan's Little Italy is dimly lit. From the shadows emerges the image of a Mafia don seated at his desk, straight from *The Godfather*. It is Marlon Brando, reading the evening newspaper.

ANGLE ON BRANDO/THE DON

ANGLE ON MATTHEW BRODERICK/CLARK KELLOGG

Broderick is Clark Kellogg, a clean-cut American lad. He approaches The Don's desk, his eyes riveted on Brando. He is led by The Don's nephew, played by Bruno Kirby, who also played the young Clemenza in *The Godfa-*

ther, Part II. Kirby/Nephew introduces Broderick/ Kellogg to Brando/The Don.

BRODERICK/KELLOGG
(to Brando/The Don)
You know, you look just like the God...

KIRBY/NEPHEW
(interrupting Broderick/Kellogg)
Clark, you never told me your last name.

BRODERICK/KELLOGG
Kellogg.

BRANDO/THE DON
Just like the cereal. Like the breakfast cereal.

(Following some polite conversation about espresso and a photograph of Mussolini hanging on his wall, Brando/The Don smiles.)

BRANDO/THE DON
How'd you like a nut?

(He offers Broderick/Kellogg a bowl of walnuts. More polite conversation.)

BRANDO/THE DON
My nephew tells me you're from Kansas.

BRODERICK/KELLOGG
Vermont.

KIRBY/NEPHEW
Six of one, half a dozen of the other.

BRANDO/THE DON
Kansas, Vermont...you know, the most important thing is that we're all Americans. That's right?

BRODERICK/KELLOGG
That's right.

CUT TO REALITY

The preceding is an embellished, telescoped transcript of a scene from Andrew Bergman's *The Freshman*. Like the 1990 film itself, the transcript conflates characters with the actors who play them, to prove a point about mainstream (white) America's collective cultural consciousness. The point is that Italian Americans are no longer high on the list of ethnic and racial groups who frighten America. Still, when they interact with Italian Americans in real life, many Americans like Clark Kellogg continue to associate them with screen images of mafiosi. The truth is that mafiosi, Italian American criminals and brutes, remain as much a part of American culture as cowboys, or, better, Indians; it's just that, over time, these original gangsters have come to appear tame, familiar, domestic, and in some cases rather white, especially compared with other threats: Asian mafias, Jamaican posses, Arab terrorists, Columbian drug lords, and those old stand-by imaginary villains, non-singing African American men.

Sometime in the mid-1970s, on an episode of *The Carroll Burnett Show*, Steve Lawrence donned a pinstripe suit, shoved wads of cotton in his cheeks, and played a bumbling, mumbling Mafia don. From roughly that time on, the Godfather mystique would never be the same. A decade later, the mafioso as stock comic character had ascended to the right hand of mafioso as stock dramatic character. As much as an American symbol of alien power, he had become an

American symbol of alien power mocked. Former child actor Dean Stockwell as Tony "The Tiger" Russo in Jonathan Demme's 1988 film *Married to the Mob* took his place next to newly-made mob boss John Gotti. Marlon Brando as Carmine "The Toucan" Sabatini in *The Freshman* sat face to face with his younger self as Don Vito Corleone.

As fear often begets laughter, and familiarity breeds mockery, so America's making the mafia comedic may have been inevitable, a part of the process of cultural acceptance (Davies qtd in Mintz 25), akin to that of turning the angry Black man or inhumanly stoic Indian into humorous figures. To the American mind, the mafioso went from fearsome criminal to semi-articulate, buffoonish goon, lovable outlaw.

Since the mid-1980s, comic screen mobsters have ranged from Jack Nicholson's raffish, sympathetic Charlie Partana in *Prizzi's Honor* to Dom DeLuise's in every sense ridiculous Don Calzone (a.k.a. "The Oddfather") in the 1998 straight-to-video flop, *The Godson*. In each case, the mafioso, still the most visible representative of Italian Americans in the media, is a subject of comic derision. The American public loves to laugh at him for what Aristotle would call his "flaws" or "ugliness," which are funny because they are not "painful or injurious" to the audience (10). These flaws (physical, mental or moral) include indifference, even enthusiasm for violence, inability to control passions, amoral familism, and contempt for American society's institutions. Instead of inspiring fear and loathing (and admiration, as in *The Godfather* films and other outlaw flicks), these deficiencies now inspire laughter.

Mafiosi have become the subject of humor for several reasons. From World War II until the 1970s, Italian American organized crime families, structured and run more like corporations than actually families, wielded immeasurable power in American cities, sometimes through overt intimidation, but more often through the covert corruption of American political institutions (Mobilio 1). Through films such as *The Godfather* and *The Godfather, Part II,* the Mafia came to be both feared for their brutality and admired for their efficiency. In admiring mafiosi, the public (including many Italian Americans) have also come to identify with them (Vecoli 55). Over the past two decades, as the Mafia's power has crumbled, as the federal government has cracked down on Italian American organized crime (2), and as other ethnic organized crime groups have muscled in on their turf, the mafia's public image has become less fearsome and tragic, more sympathetic and comic.

The 1998 Mafia comedy *Analyze This* takes stock of these changes. When a friendly capo remarks to Don Paul Vitti (Robert DeNiro), that "made guys are goin' to the feds," and "then you got the Chinese and the crazy Russians"; that, in short, "things are changin," Vitti sardoncially replies, "Whaddya want me to do, open a website?" Ultimately, Vitti finds that his only way to keep up is to get out. Thankfully, the script's semi-sophistication keeps him from parroting Don Michael Corleone's famous line from *The Godfather, Part III,* "Just when I thought I was out, they pull me back in." (Paulie Walnuts, a Mafia henchman in HBO's absolutely sophisticated series, "The Sopranos," does repeat the line, but only so that the show's creator, David Chase, can make a point about the Mafia's late-stage self-consciousness and their own ironic awareness of the mafioso's place in American culture.)

It is easy to identify with Vitti's dilemma, but not with his character. Americans often experience stress on the job, brought on by competition and the need to update their skill sets, but they rarely face Vitti's specific problems, and are generally not homicidal. Vitti weeps, seeks out an analyst, and reveals secrets of his childhood, but he is never thoughtful or admirable. At one point, after a brief introductory session with Doctor Sobel (Billy Crystal), Vitti warns the analyst, "If I go fag, you die"; and after a subsequent nervous episode, tells him that his advice "didn't take." At no time does Vitti appear to be anything more than a selfish goon with a problem, an object of parody.

Parody leaves characters flat and makes them appear ridiculous shadows of human beings. Anyone concerned with the public image of Italian Americans may see Vitti's parodic flatness as a blessing or a curse. On one hand, a sympathetic mafioso will only broaden the appeal of the mafioso image, and in the bargain make mafiosi, and by extension Italian Americans, appear less than human beings. On the other hand, a parodic mafioso will disarm and demystify the mafioso (and Italian Americans). To weigh its merits and to understand the significance of Mafia comedy, we have to consider the nature of comedy itself—comedy of derision versus comedy of identification.

While it may involve a degree of audience identification with its object, parody is essentially comedy of derision. It derides its subject, without seeking to reform it; so it attacks more gently than satire (Hill 221). And it has proven the rule of Mafia comedy, recasting even as it cements (slight pun intended) the screen image of the mafioso. We must ask then, does the development of the parodic mafioso represent progress for the public image of Italian Americans?

The American public now identifies Italian Americans with parodic Mafiosi, as do many Italian Americans themselves, like the fictional Italian American Nick Shay (who is, by trade, a waste management consultant, what Tony Soprano purports to be) in Don DeLillo's 1997 novel *Underworld*, who performs comic mafioso impersonations for his non-Italian American colleagues. Through Mafia parody, Italian Americans continue to be identified and to identify themselves with cold-blooded criminals, but criminals who are ridiculous—less than human and less powerful than before. The rise of Mafia parody is especially unfortunate, because it parallels the real-life integration of Italian Americans into an ever-widening variety of American geographical regions, ethnic groups, social classes, and professions (Monti 24-26). For example, a number of Italian Americans can count themselves among America's leading filmmakers.

Fortunately, some Italian American filmmakers have recognized the cultural currency of the mafioso figure, and in their films have attempted to humanize him and use him as a means of Italian American cultural expression. In spite of Mafia comedies such as *The Don's Analyst* (1997), *The Godson* (1998), *Jane Austen's Mafia* (1999), *Analyze This* (1999), and *Mickey Blue Eyes* (1999)—a Mafia comedy of identification has also had its day; it is a brand of comedy that presents complex characters in mundane American situations, with whom and with which general American audiences can identify. Americans now can laugh with the Mafia—and with Italian Americans—instead of laughing at them. And an audience who laughs with, rather than at, the comic subject will be more receptive to cultural messages sent through that subject.

The first Mafia comedy of identification was Martin Scorsese's *Goodfellas*. Its characters demonstrate a wit and emotional complexity, if not always an intelligence, previously foreign to the Mafia genre. These Italian and Irish American gangsters not only have two families, but they also interact with the members of their families in ways that make them appear at times glamorous, at times ridiculous, and at times ordinary. Yes, Jimmy Conway (DeNiro) and Tommy DeSimone (Joe Pesci) indulge in hyper-violent murder, and, yes, they commandeer shipments like Old West stagecoach robbers—during one such robbery, Tommy points his gun in a victimized truck driver's face and yells, "Where's the strongbox, you fuckin' varmint?"—but these same swashbuckling gangsters also sell cigarettes from the trunks of cars, vacation on the Jersey shore, dine in tacky restaurants, live in still tackier houses, and with the exception of weekly trysts with girlfriends, enjoy mundane domestic lives. Their lives are familiar not only to Italian Americans, but also to most Americans.

These outlaw citizens are living symbols of Italian American cultural traits with which Italian Americans and non-Italian Americans alike can identify; they are symbols of Italian American assimilation. When Tommy and the boys stop by his mother's house at 2 a. m. for a shovel, which they need to bury a body stowed in the trunk of their car, his mother, *all'italo-americana*, is there waiting with a full meal. She urges Tommy to "get a nice girl, so you can settle down," and then tells a funny story that "in Italian... sounds much nicer." Her story itself is a symbol: a story of the stock Italian comic figure, the cuckold (D'Acierno 612). The Italian American signs in this scene may only be intelligible to an Italian American audience in touch with its heritage, but the mild mother-son antagonism is recognizable to any American audience; it is a scene of family—similar to a number of scenes from *The Godfather* movies and films—with which they can identify.

It may appear that films like *Goodfellas* do more harm than good for the public image of Italian Americans. The Italian American man as mobster remains an anti-social American (Talese, qtd. in Haberman B1); however, his tendency toward sociopathy makes sense (in some small degree, at least) to any American who has never wanted to play that other stock comic type, the little soul, the schlemiel, to callous corporations and bureaucracies, or to the kind of mind-numbing life Henry Hill (Ray Liotta), the most Americanized of the Goodfellas, is doomed to live.

Tony Soprano, of David Chase (DeCesare)'s HBO series *The Sopranos*, appears to be an Italian American sociopath, even though in many ways he is a regular American Joe. The series opens with a shot of Tony lying flat on his back, speaking in voice-over to his therapist, Doctor Jennifer Melfi (Lorraine Bracco, who also played Karen Hill in *Goodfellas*), remarking, "It's good to be in something from the ground floor. I came too late for that, I know. But lately I'm getting the feeling that I came in at the end. The best is over." In both his personal and professional lives, Tony suffers various symbolic forms of castration, hence his last name. As Mafia don, he contends with his resentful uncle (archly named "Junior") who puts a contract out on him, and a gang of incompetent or subversive subordinates. His nephew Christopher Moltisanti (Michael Imperioli, who also played Spider in *Goodfellas*), one of his soldiers, writes and ultimately produces a screenplay about Mafia life; one of his most trusted *paesans*, Big Pussy Bonpensero (Vincent Pastore), turns government informant; and the brother of the former family boss, the ruthless Richie Aprile (David Proval), openly defies his authority. And the list Tony's bêtes noires goes on.

As son, husband, father, and brother, Tony's power is even more dubious. Livia, his mother (Nancy Marchand), strongly suggests to Uncle Junior (Dominic Chianese) that he be killed, and continually undercuts his attempts to discipline his children and run his business. At the dinner table, as the family debates how Anthony, Junior (Robert Iler) ought to be disciplined for misbehaving in church and school, Livia blurts out, "His father was the same way. I practically lived in the principal's office." Other women too challenge Tony's traditional position as patriarch of the Italian American family. When he tries to teach his children a lesson about Italian tradition, the historical contributions of Italians, his daughter Meadow (Jamie-Lynn Sigler) asks smartly, "Who invented the Mafia?" And when his sister Janice (Aida Turturro) returns to New Jersey from Seattle, she forces him to lift a retaliatory ban on discussion of Livia in the Soprano household, and interferes in the punishment of his daughter. Later, this same sister pre-empts his strike on her boyfriend, the insubordinate soldier Aprile. Not to mention Doctor Melfi's influence.

Whenever Tony argues with his wife, she stops him dead with complaints about his extra-marital affairs and failure to show her affection. On the latter count, Tony, like his Uncle Junior, is not entirely guilty. He often hugs Carmella and kisses her affectionately, but he only rarely makes love to her and rarely shows affection in public. Uncle Junior, meanwhile, is madly in love with his long-time girlfriend, until word gets out to him that she has been talking publicly of his prowess at cunnilingus, at which point Junior smashes a pie in her face and walks out on her forever. Their behavior with their women indicates that both Tony and Junior, although they belong to the economic middle class, wrestle with the traditional, working-class, Italian American male code of romantic conduct. According to that code, to be overly sentimental, sensitive, affectionate, or submissive with a woman shows intolerable weakness (Gambino 145). When a symbolic intra-family Mafia war breaks out, Tony remarks to Doctor Melfi, "Cunnilingus and psychotherapy brought us to this." Departure from the traditional codes threatens Italian American unity and (male) identity. It also signifies a shift from to middle- and upper-middle-class Italian American identity, for which the working-class ethic of their organization has poorly prepared these mafiosi. Still, the family conflict does not deter Tony from analysis; and we may safely assume that it will not deter Uncle Junior from oral sex. Both men represent contemporary versions of Italian American male identity, versions that challenge received macho screen images of Italian American men, who, in reality, struggle and often fail to live up to those images.

Like millions of Americans, Tony is undergoing psychotherapy. As an "old school" (his term) Italian American man, Tony should keep his mouth shut to EVERYONE about family business, but he breaks the code of silence, *omertà,* when he visits Doctor Melfi. Through Junior's and Livia's disgust with Tony's therapy, his "weakness," the American audience comes to understand the rules of this code and the consequences (expulsion from the family, death) of violating those rules. The audience can also sympathize with Tony's plight as surburbanite on the couch. Therapist/patient exchanges strike a chord (often a comic chord) with the audience. These exchanges are, therefore, ideal media for the comic expression and translation of Italian American ideas and values, in Italian American language; and for an airing of the internecine Italian American debate over the identity (as above) and public image of Italian Americans (Alaya). In one of his early sessions with Melfi, Tony voices a skepticism of psychotherapy and its jargon, a skepticism common among Italian Americans, when he yells, "Dysfunction, *va fa'n'cul'* [up your ass]." The language and the sentiment are specifically Italian American, but the frustration with therapy-speak and the audacious expression of that frustration is common.

Caught between his mother, his wife, his children, and his crime family, Tony admits to Melfi, "No matter what I do, I feel guilty." The Italian American doctor's response cuts to the heart of Italian American male identity: "You accord this little old lady [your mother] an almost mystical ability to wreak havoc." Doctor Melfi's diagnosis emerges from the combination of training and intimate cultural knowledge. She is a psychoanalyst trained in America and dressed in business attire; she uses the methods of her American profession to approach problems. She is also, however, an Italian American woman familiar with the power structure of the Italian American family; she recognizes the typical Italian American mother-son relationship, which is common enough among the general population: the domineering mother, the resentful but devoted son. With a pained expression on his face, Tony comes to Livia's defense. "She's a good woman. She put food on that table every night." What we see of Livia Soprano as a potentially lethal younger mother—At one point, in a flashback sequence, she brandishes a kitchen knife and tells young Tony that she should stab him in the heart—belies Tony's defense. From her children she exacts the high price of security and self-esteem. Her behavior as a young mother, like her later suggestion that Tony be clipped, demonstrates that the Italian American model of woman's self-sacrifice for the men of the family (Bona 207, 210-213) camouflages the true order of Italian American society, which is, to borrow Luigi Barzini's term for Italy, a "crypto-matriarchy" (202). In the series' second season, this matriarchy emerges from the shadows in the form of an Italian donna, a woman Mafia boss, Donna Annalisa (Sofia Milos), and, more powerfully, in the form of a steeled Carmella.

Only in his leisure time does Tony appear completely in control. He lives the life of the immature, irresponsible bachelor, the pampered only son (though we learn that as a child he was not this), and the wayward, ne'er-do-well husband, a stock type of Italian and Italian American culture, and increasingly, of American culture. He spends much of his spare time at a strip club called Bada Bing! and some of it with his impudent Russian American mistress or unstable Italian American mistress, aboard his boat named The Stugots-"*stugots*," a phonetic rendition of the Southern Italian dialect "*stu'cazz'*," or "*test'u'cazz'*" equivalent of the Standard Italian, "*testa di cazzo*," in English, "dickhead." In other words, Tony revels in the role of (Italian) American playboy, despite having a wife, two children, and a house in the suburbs. He is the casual patriarch both of an Italian American family secretly run by women and of a post-War American "dream" that squelched women's subtle power only by force of unreal prosperity and then only for a brief historical moment. His real power lies only in escape from these institutions, though even this escape is jeopardized by women who have sexual power over him.

"The Sopranos," of course, does not have a monopoly on the humorous combination of Mafia don and psychoanalyst. In his parody of Mafia psychotherapy, *Analyze This,* Ivan Reitman uses therapy to perpetuate the mafioso character type and so perpetuate Italian American stereotypes. Reitman's don emerges from analysis as a selfish, good-hearted (Shepard 27), but unremorseful brute, who is simply worn out from having to contend with "cunning" "animals" (rival mafiosi) and bumbling goons (his henchmen). Through therapy and other forms of able assistance from his establishment Jewish American psychiatrist, Doctor Sobel (Billy Crystal), Don Vitti escapes his criminal world, to live happily ever after in civilian America, without having to live as a schlemiel. At a climactic meeting of the dons, Sobel quells a rebellion against Don Vitti, by putting his rival, Primo (Chazz Palmintieri), on the couch. When Primo begins to yell about Vitti's absence, Sobel asks him, "Do you feel you have to get angry to be heard, so people will listen to you?" When Vitti finally arrives, he informs the other mafiosi that he is "in a good place right now" and wants to retire, and instead of killing a turncoat underling, advises him, to "Look inside the inner self and find out who you are." Don Vitti, the Italian American killer, has suddenly taken on an air of rectitude, and in his place has arisen Paul Vitti. He has apparently become the assimilated disciple of American psychotherapy, though he neither repents nor pays for his crimes.

By freeing the don from his Italian American family, *Analyze This* imposes the middle class values of American psychiatry on the lowest social class of Italian Americans. In spite of Vitti's protests ("Freud was a sick fuck, and you are too!"), and Doctor Sobel's temporary need to resort to violence, in the end analysis triumphs over *onore*; paternalistic white American rationality over puerile Italian American irrationality. We are left with a miraculously converted, chastened, unredeemed, flat Italian American hero, and with a denigrating outcome.

More episodic than *Analyze This*, more like a novel, and genuinely comedic, *The Sopranos* allows Italian American culture to answer the charges that American culture brings against it. Tony Soprano often has an Italian American answer to his more assimilated analyst's American therapy-speak. Tony, one Italian American, continually reminds Doctor Melfi, another Italian American, of her *italianità*. In an early episode, glimpsing the name on her diploma, he asks her, "What part of the boot you from, Hon?" As it happens, she is not from the same part (Avellino) as he, but in America, he implies, to resist discrimination, and cultural loss, Italians must stick together and remind each other of who they are. Tony consistently stresses the importance of this cultural identification, while still participating in mainstream American activities such as attending his daughter's soccer games and meeting with the principal of his son's school. His sense of Italian American identity and participation in the dominant culture together represent a viable social alternative to Don Vitti's empty conversion.

In two of its many dinner scenes, *The Sopranos* presents a scene of Tony's family discussing the historical contributions of Italians and Italian Americans, alongside a scene of Doctor Melfi's family (who do not have organized crime standing between them and the American upper-middle class) debating the humanity of mobsters and the deleterious effect their presence has on the public image of Italian Americans. Following a FBI search of the Soprano house, which the feds derisively refer to as "the sausage factory," Tony complains about a certain Agent Grasso. "What's he think, he's gonna make it to the top by arresting his own people?" Tony exclaims. "He'll learn. He'll see." When Tony mentions the vowel at the end of Grasso's name, Anthony, Junior says, "We have a vowel," to which Tony replies, "F'in right, and you be proud of it. Jesus Christ, you'd think there never was a Michelangelo, the way they treat people." By "they," Tony means the *"Merigan',"* mainstream Americans. His use of "they" indicates that this discussion of "them" is meant for Italian Americans only. Here are Italian American points-of-view on American prejudice. The conversation that follows reflects these points-of-view. Carmella asks, "Did you know that an Italian invented the telephone." Anthony, Junior, in his cultural ignorance, responds, "Alexander Graham Bell was Italian?" And Tony, the mafioso as cultural conduit, retorts, "You see what I'm talking about?...Antonio Meucci invented the telephone, and he was robbed! Everybody knows that!"

Around the Melfi family table, discussion centers on Tony, who, as a patient (and symbolic mafioso), must remain anonymous in conversation. When Doctor Melfi hints she may have a mafioso patient, her mother worries, "I just hope he's not one of those crumbs they're talking about on the news." Her ex-husband Richard (Richard Romanus) interjects, "He's scum, and you shouldn't help him with his bed-wetting." The doctor, who has dealt with Tony across the lines of class and law, as one Italian American to another, defends him. But Richard, an Italian American anti-defamation activist, gives her no quarter. "People like him are the reason Italian Americans have such a bad image," he declares. "Ask any American to describe an Italian American in this country, and invariably he's gonna reference *The Godfather, Goodfellas*... and the rest of them are gonna mention pizza." Doctor Melfi's college-age son Jason (Will McCormack)—who by virtue of his generation and privilege has had less reason to fret over anti-Italian American bias—then quips, "Good movies to eat pizza by," but Richard continues his protest. "Why do you think we're never going to see an Italian President." Doctor Melfi again defends Tony as a human being, replying, "I realize that you're involved in the anti-defamation lobby, so go after Hollywood if you feel you absolutely have to. Leave my patient alone." Still, Richard, the baby boomer, Italian American intellectual, attacks. "It's a synergy. News items and the constant portrayal of Italian Americans as gangsters." The debate grows more complex (as it generally has among Italian American intellectuals), when Jason remarks, "Wasn't the Italian anti-def deal started by Joe Colombo, a mobster?" Ignoring this subtlety, Richard, the crusader, laments that the infinitesimal "fraction" of the Italian American population who have been mafiosi (5,000) have cast "a dark shadow over twenty million hard-working Americans." Although he recognizes discrimination, Richard is quick to defend the profound Americanness of Italian Americans, as most Italian Americans would. Unimpressed, more comfortable in his skin, Jason answers, "Dad, at this point in our [American] cultural history, mob movies are classic American cinema, like Westerns." Representing the dismissal of Italian American cultural activism, Doctor Melfi's father, Joseph (Bill Richardone) chimes in, "I have to agree there, Rich, You never saw the Scotch-Irish pissin' and moanin' about being portrayed as rustlers and gunslingers," to which her mother responds, "That's absurd."

The Melfi's debate reflects the state of cultural awareness of many middle and upper-class Italian Americans these days. These are the people who belong to groups such as the National Italian American

Foundation and other organizations dedicated to the promotion of Italian American culture and the enhancement of Italian American public image.

These serio-comic discussions are unique in American film and television. They expose a vast American audience to two of the *discorsi,* the points of argument, that for the past several decades have occupied not only Italian Americans like Richard, but also producers and scholars of Italian American culture. In the process, they reflect a variety of Italian American views on the place and image of Italian Americans. They also reveal Chase and his writers as Italian American artists who question their own use of the mafioso image to create Italian American popular culture, a phenomenon until recently limited, as Richard suggests, to Italian food, vicious criminals, and chaotic families. These discussions can exist on television, because *The Sopranos* enjoys not only critical acclaim (21 Emmy Awards and 111 nominations), but also and especially because it enjoys wild popularity (Mifflin E27), a popularity that derives probably from its superb writing (the popularity of less well-written shows may prove otherwise) and certainly from its subject matter, the Italian American Mafia, unfortunately still the most recognizable and widely appealing symbol of Italian American culture.

Should we then try to transform this symbol, as Chase, and to some degree Scorsese, have done? Should we ignore it? Should we protest it? Certainly, protests such as Bill Dal Cerro's impassioned article "Hollywood vs. Italians" have a place, but to change America's collective consciousness mind by mind, we need to control our own myths (Valerio, Interview with Lopate)—in this case, by "we" I mean producers of Italian American art and commentary. Rather than just complain about the stereotyping, we need to call attention to the role that economic and social class have played in the construction of stereotypes, and insist upon a diversity of Italian American images before the public gaze.

American history indicates that although protest may win civil rights, it will not necessarily convince white America that its stereotypes of the people it fears do not exist. It may even cause Americans to react by, metaphorically speaking, thrusting malapropisms, pinstriped suits, and heaping bowls of spaghetti and meatballs in Italian American faces. (Watermelon-wielding Italian Americans themselves reacted in a similar way to African Americans during Al Sharpton's 1989 protest of the killing of Yusuf Hawkins). Derogatory remarks about Italian American will be given voice and form, then simply go underground. History also indicates that overcoming stereotypes often requires the preliminary step of making them comical—transforming monstrous images into human images. Italian American artists must, however, dictate the terms of that transformation, as they have begun to do. I'm suggesting that the new Mafia comedy of identification may represent a final phase and an artistic appropriation of the mafioso myth. If Italian American writers and filmmakers leave this myth to mainstream America, we will get Dom DeLuise as a moronic Don Calzone hitting his son for no reason and telling him, "It's the Italian way. I'm expressing love." But if mafiosi are portrayed as ordinary schlemiels, and if they convey real Italian American values and ideas to a national audience, then as media figures they will cease to fascinate the American public for the wrong reasons, cease to inspire public ridicule of Italian Americans, and in the process will do us a valuable service. They will clear the screen for a spectrum of rounded, human Italian American characters, and for varied, realistic projections of Italian American experience.

Works Cited

Alaya, Flavia. "Re: Mafia Comedy Paper." E-mail to the author. 5 Dec. 1999.

Analyze This. Dir. Ivan Reitman. Perf. Robert DeNiro, Billy Crystal. Warner Brothers, 1999.

Aristotle. *On Poetry and Style.* Trans. G. M. A. Grube. Indiana: Bobbs-Merrill Educational Publishing, 1958.

Barzini, Luigi. *The Italians.* New York: Atheneum, 1964.

Bona, Mary Jo. "On Being an Italian American Woman." *The Italian American Heritage.*

Ed. Pellegrino D'Acierno. New York: Garland Publishing, 1999.

D'Acierno, Pellegrino. "Cinema Paradiso: The Italian American Presence in American Cinema."

The Italian American Heritage. Ed. Pellegrino D'Acierno. New York: Garland Publishing, 1999.

Dal Cerro, Bill. "Hollywood vs. Italians." *Fra Noi.* Jan. 1999: 54-56.

DeLillo, Don. *Underworld.* New York: Scribner, 1997.

The Freshman. Dir. Andrew Bergman. Perf. Marlon Brando, Matthew Broderick, and Bruno Kirby. Tri-Star, 1990.

Gambino, Richard. *Blood of My Blood: The Dilemma of the Italian Americans.* Garden City: Anchor Books, 1975.

The Godfather. Dir. Francis Ford Coppola. Perf. Marlon Brando, James Caan, and Al Pacino. Paramount, 1972.

The Godfather, Part II. Dir. Francis Ford Coppola. Perf. Al Pacino, Robert DeNiro, and Diane Keaton.

The Godfather, Part III. Dir. Francis Ford Coppola. Perf. Al Pacino, Diane Keaton.

The Godson. Perf. Don DeLuise, 1998.

Goodfellas. Dir. Martin Scorsese. Perf. Robert DeNiro, Joe Pesci. Warner Brothers, 1990.

Haberman, Clyde. "A Stereotype Hollywood Can't Refuse." *New York Times.* 30 July 1999, early ed.: B1.

Hill, Hamlin. "The Future of American Humor: Through a Glass Eye Darkly." *Critical Essays on American Humor*. Ed. William Bedford Clark. Boston, G.K. Hall & Co., 1984. 219-226.

Lawrence, Steve, perf. *The Carroll Burnett Show*. Perf. Carroll Burnett, Harvey Korman, and Tim Conway. CBS. WCBS, New York, 1973.

Married to the Mob. Dir Jonathan Demme. Perf. Dean Stockwell, Michelle Pfeiffer. Orion, 1988.

Mifflin, Lawrie. "In a Coup for Cable, HBO's 'Sopranos' Receives 16 Emmy Nominations." *New York Times*. 23 July 1999, early ed.: E27.

Mintz, Lawrence E. "Humor and Ethnic Stereotypes in Vaudeville and Burlesque." *MELUS*. 21.4 (1996): 19-28.

Mobilio, Albert. "Why Organized Crime Isn't What it Used to Be." *The Village Voice Online* 29 Sept.-5 Oct., 1999. 25 Jan. 2000 <http://www.villagevoice.com/issues/9939/mobilio.shtml>.

Monti, Daniel J., Jr. "The Working and Reworking of Italian-American Ethnicity in the United States." *Italian Americans in a Multicultural Society*. Ed. Jerome Krase and Judith N. DeSena. Stony Brook, NY: Forum Italicum, 1994. 19-34.

Shepherd, Jim. "A Wry Look at the Days When a Don was a Don." *New York Times*. 4 April 1999, early ed.: 27.

The Sopranos. Creat., David Chase. Perf. James Gandolfini, Nancy Marchand, Lorraine Bracco, Edy Falco. Various episodes. HBO. 1999-2000.

Valerio, Anthony. Interview with Leonard Lopate. *New York and Company*. Natl. Public Radio. WNYC, New York. 7 August 1997.

Vecoli, Rudolph J. "The Search for an Italian American Identity." *Rivista di studi anglo-americani* 3 (1984): 29-65.

Two Mafia Cinemas
A Review Essay

American mafia movies like *The Godfather* (Francis Ford Coppola, 1972) have highlighted the operation of individual mafiosi within criminal organizations and against American law and law enforcement. In so doing, they have mostly ignored the organizations' negative impact on American society. This approach has tended to humanize mafiosi characters, to mythologize them as outlaw heroes, and to create a collective mafia movie tale from their points of view.

Italian mafia films have, on the other hand, been more concerned with social justice than with the use of genre to create appealing mafiosi characters and to sustain mafia mythology. These films have tended to present narratives whose protagonists are law enforcement officials, brave citizens or others who must confront the constant menace of the mafia. The collective Italian mafia film tale is primarily a story of anti-mafia activism.

The difference in these two mafia cinemas reflects two divergent national experiences of the mafia (the term used here to encompass various Italian American and Italian criminal organizations). This difference is the overarching theme of Dana Renga's anthology *Mafia Movies: A Reader*, and of her introductory survey of the volume's territory. The volume is divided into three parts of unequal length: "Setting the Scene," "American Mafia Movies: The Corleones at Home and Abroad" and "Italian Mafia Movies: Myth and Resistance." Renga's survey, which leads Part I, the briefest of the three, like many of the volume's essays, is concise and incisive (even if Renga's prose is marred now and then by clumsy turns of phrase (for example, "Giuliano becomes a tragic figure as he attempts to exact change in a land where nothing changes"). In Part Two of the collection, Vincenzo Maggitti and Joanne Ruvoli write of the earliest American mafia movies, produced during the first two decades of the twentieth century, which were also the last two decades of mass Italian immigration to the United States. During this era the print media and nascent film industry tended to portray Italian immigrants, and mafiosi especially, as serious threats to society. These portrayals begin with the 1906 Biograph short, *The Black Hand* (Wallace McCutcheon), and continue with several D. W. Griffith Biograph films that take Italian Americans as their subjects. In their well-wrought essays, Maggitti and Ruvoli demonstrate how these short films include 'good' and 'bad' Italians, how they present non-Anglo ethnicity as a force antithetical to assimilation and thus to the public good. The sum of this equation is the 'classical' gangster films of the early 1930s. Of these *Little Ceasar* (Mervyn LeRoy, 1931) and *Scarface* (Brian De Palma, 1983) stand above the rest, and are here skillfully scrutinized by Norma Bouchard, whose "Ethnicity and the classical gangster movie," like Maggitti's essay, builds on Peter Bonadella's indispensable survey, *Hollywood Italians: Dagos, Palookas, Romeos, Wise Guys, and Sopranos* (Continuum, 2009).

Bonadella's history of the Hays code explains why and how it prevented the production of most Italian American mafia films from 1934 until the mid-1960s. In his contribution to the volume, Robert Casillo, with his customary élan, also discusses the code's impact, and exhumes Martin Ritt's *The Brotherhood* (1968) (an interesting but mildly risible Kirk Douglas vehicle), to show how Ritt's film, along with the advent of the rating system, paved the way for Francis Ford Coppola. Coppola's *The Godfather*, based on Mario Puzo's 1969 novel, is the first American film to present emotionally complex mafiosi characters.

A number of critics have described the Corleones as thoughtful outlaws, whose ethnic unity has appealed to an audience experiencing a fragmentation of mainstream American identity; while their ethnic difference and violence (phenomena closely associated in mafia films) set them apart as undesirable and menacing, though not gravely threatening to public order. As Chris Messenger argues in his 2002 volume, *The Godfather and American Culture: How the Corleones Became "Our Gang"* (SUNY Press), the Corleones essentially create the mafia mythology we know today. For Messenger, *The Godfather* is "the inadvertent epic of American immigration." Anthony Tamburri's essay in the present volume, "Michael Corleone's Tie," also reads *The Godfather* as an immigrant "saga," through the semantics of wardrobe. While Tamburri's essay is among the most original here, Renga could have included more than one essay on what is essentially *the* seminal film of the genre as contemporary audiences know it. As an Italian Americanist, I was surprised to see only one essay on Coppola's master cinematic text. This may say as much about scholars' tastes circa 2012 as it does about anything else, and perhaps we have reached the end of—or a hiatus in—the fetishization of this film.

For this and other reasons, anyone reading *Mafia Movies: A Reader* would profit from also reading George Laake-Walsh's *Screening the Mafia: Masculinity, Ethnicity and Mobsters from* The Godfather *to* The Sopranos (McFarland and Company, 2010). Laake-Walsh claims that *The Godfather* tells its immigrant story through generic language established by earlier films but only fully developed and promulgated by Coppola's gangster trilogy and other films of the "post-classical" era. The cinematic vocabulary of post-classical mafia films casts the mafioso as an alternative model of American manhood (and, metaphorically, of American power), whose behaviour and ethnicity audiences can by turns admire or deplore. Fred Gardaphé makes a similar point in his book *From Wiseguys to Wise Men: The Gangster and Italian American Masculinities* (Routledge, 2006). For Gardaphé, the mafioso of American film, as an essential trickster figure, shows us "both what is and is not American and what is and is not acceptable behaviour" for men in American society.

Several other essays here take up the theme of corruption, at the heart of many post-*Godfather* mafia movies. As John Paul Russo suggests in his sophisticated and poetic contribution to the present volume on *The Godfather: Part II* (Francis Ford Coppola, 1974), the mafiosi protagonists of later mafia films are perhaps honorable and perhaps redeemable. Several of the critics in *Mafia Movies* make strong cases for the importance of seldom acknowledged recent mafia films (the most credible of these being Lara Santoro, through her discussion of gender relations in Abel Ferrara's unsung *The Funeral,* 1996). Still, it would seem that the most influential mafia films after *The Godfather* trilogy remain *Goodfellas* (Martin Scorsese 1990), *Donnie Brasco* (Mike Newell, 1997), and *The Sopranos* (David Chase, 1999-2007). (The television series *The Untouchables* and *The Sopranos* are discussed as extended films.) As the commentators in this collection suggest, all of these films explore the fate of compromised mafiosi, men who, no matter how strongly they believe in mafia mythology, can no longer live it, in the wake of the RICO act and the disintegration and disfiguration of *omertà* and of Italian ethnicity.

In his essay "Martin Scorsese's *Goodfellas*: Hybrid Storytelling Between Realism and Formalism," Fulvio Orsitto observes the ways in which *Goodfellas* sets the dissonant tone, simultaneously sustaining and deconstructing mafia myths through Scorsese's choice of voice-over narration. Ray Liotta's deadpan delivery exposes the sordid reality of the heretofore glamourous American movie mafioso. As Orsitto observes, the film's use of a woman (Karen Hill, played by Lorraine Bracco, who also animates *The Sopranos*' Jennifer Melfi) as a central character brings to American mafia cinema an Italian reformist sensibility. This point is not lost on Jane and Peter Schneider in their slight but suitable introductory essay on gender and violence in Part One of the volume. In praising Scorsese's reformist impulses, Orsitto understates, however, the director's contribution to mafioso glamour, through comedy and star power in the persons of Robert De Niro and Joe Pesci. In *Screening the Mafia*, Laake-Walsh examines at great length this exploitation of familiar faces, describing Al Pacino as the archetypal America mafia actor, cast in various films not only for his (sometimes hyperbolic) acting ability, but for his value as a signifier of mafia myths constructed by earlier films. In his essay here on *The Sopranos*, Franco Ricci remarks that mafia iconography guides compromised mafiosi like Tony Soprano, who becomes, to his detriment and to our delight, a man as much of words as of action. Tony's evolution reflects the evolution of the genre itself, from, in Laake-Walsh's words, Coppola's "golden glow" to Scorsese's "neon glare"; from gangster epic, to, as Orsitto phrases it, "gangster demythification"; and finally, from melodrama to satire.

Evident from a reading of the collection's second part, is that the transformation of the American mafia genre has resulted, in great measure, from the decline of the American mafia, and has fed on its own byproduct: the growing status of mafiosi as stylish icons. Their numen is nostalgia for white ethnic male power; yet, ironically, these mafiosi have also become paragons for gangsta rap artists and other media bad boys. The most comprehensive and liveliest account of the mafia myth's popular culture currency is George DeStefano's *An Of-*

fer We Can't Refuse: The Mafia in the Mind of America (Faber and Faber, 2006). DeStefano's book, written for a general audience, is especially valuable for its exploration of the myth's impact on Italian Americans and of its implications for (Italian) American masculinity. As a contributor to Part Three of Renga's volume, which is dedicated to films about the mafia produced in Italy, DeStefano calls our attention to the destructive effects of the male honour code on Italian boys in areas controlled by the Camorra and other criminal groups, effects portrayed in films such as Marco Risi's *Mery per sempre/Mary Forever* (1989), Antonio and Andrea Frazzi's *Certi bambini/A Children's Story* (2004), and Matteo Garrone's *Gomorra/Gomorrah* (2008).

The current corruption of their nation's youth is indeed one reason that Italian audiences prefer to view movie mafiosi as dangerous villains rather than as relatively innocuous goons. But there are other reasons. For a century and a half, southern Italy's regional mafias have functioned as shadow governments and shadow economies, largely through intimidation. Their system of extortion and patronage, sometimes called *la piovra*, the octopus, has hamstrung regional economies (and recently the national economy) and fostered attendant criminality; but, more important, has demoralized a good portion of the Italian public, who have come to accept stagnancy and corruption as facts and ways of life. Italian writers and philosophers have long wondered how to loose southern Italian society from the death-grip of a feudalism that, since the Risorgimento, has been most conspicuously embodied by these mafias.

Only after World War II, however, did the Italian cinema begin to include stories that dramatize the dilemma posed by Gramsci's southern question. While most of the commentary on Italian films about the south and specifically about the mafia has, naturally, appeared in Italian-language publications, several previous volumes of criticism in English have taken, at least in part, Italian mafia movies as their subjects—Bonadella's *Italian Cinema: From Neorealism to the Present* (Continuum, 2002); Gian Piero Brunetta's *The History of Italian Cinema* in English translation (Princeton University Press, 2009; Einaudi, 2003); Marica Landy's *Italian Cinema: National Film Traditions* (Cambridge University Press, 2000); and John Michalczyk's *The Italian Political Filmmakers* (Fairleigh Dickinson University Press, 1986)—but none so panoptically as Renga's collection.

In a few pithy pages, Danielle Hipkins demonstrates the ways in which the earliest Italian mafia movie of the sound era, Pietro Germi's *In nome della legge/In the Name of the Law* (1949), uses the oedipal conventions of Gothic romance and the American western to portray the contest between masculine forces, the state and the mafia (manifest in Guido Schiavi, a magistrate assigned to a small Sicilian town, and Massaro Turi Passalaqua, the local capo), for control of an Italian town. Later films, such as Alberto Lattuada's *Il mafioso* (1962), which stars the great Italian comic actor Alberto Sordi, satirize that contest and mark it as a national struggle, and one inseparable from capitalism and its demand for a mobile workforce. These films, according to Nelson Moe in his essay on Lattuada's film, "play with and deconstruct the traditional dichotomy between a modern, civilised north and a traditional, backwards south." This cinematic vision of state-mafia relations has grown even more disturbing in the generation since the Maxi trials and in the wake of the Berlusconi regime. Gone, in fact, from more recent Italian mafia films are most traces of comedy.

Since the 1980s somber tragedies, such as Michele Placido's *Un eroe borghese/Ordinary Hero* (1995), about investment banker-turned-anti-corruption-trial witness Giorgio Ambrosoli, who, like the union-organizing protagonist of Pasquale Scimeca's *Placido Rizzotto* (2000), is an anti-mafia reformist hero; and reformist exposés, such as Marco Turco's *In un altro paese/Excellent Cadavers* (2005), have dominated the Italian cinematic landscape. Carlo Testa's discussion of *Un eroe borghese* is a lesson in the history of mafia corruption of the Italian state. In her essay on *Placido Rizzotto*, Amy Boylan demonstrates how the film, set in Corleone, Sicily, stands *The Godfather*'s images of honourable mafiosi on their heads. The film's screen mafiosi are simply "cowardly individuals out for personal gain"; while the film itself is "a collective memorial for all those who have fought against injustice."

Both *In un altro paese*—starring Alexander Stille as himself, the author of the eponymous best-selling book, in the process of investigating the assassination of Justices Giovanni Falcone and Paolo Borsellino—and Stefano Maria Bianchi's and Alberto Nerazzini's *La mafia è bianca* (2005) reflect the cinematic prominence and social significance of mafia documentaries in Italy. As Robin Pickering-Iazzi observes in her essay on Nerazzini, "documentary filmmaking has emerged as a 'voice' that serves the ideals of democracy," through its exposure of a "Janus-faced Mafia" that has corrupted "respectable" enterprises like the national health care system. Anna Paparcone reminds us that the crusading spirit we encounter in the recent crop of documentaries and fictionalized narratives animates earlier films such as Francesco Rosi's *Le mani sulla città/Hands Over the City* (1963), produced at a time when Italian mafias had just begun to extend their reach beyond their native provinces and regions, and when Italian film-makers were among the first to sound a national alarm.

Although the alarm has been sounding for the past half-century, the anti-mafia forces that it has mobilized have thus far, tragically, failed to break the mafia's grip. Pierpaolo Antonello's account of *Gomorra*, based on Roberto Saviano's semi-fictional book of that title, describes the film's portrayal of the Neopolitan Camorra's brutality and influence; their willingness to kill not only one another, but also petty criminals like the hapless Marco and Ciro, as well as ordinary citizens, even those as powerless as a single mother living in a Neopolitan housing project; their ability to corrupt pre-adolescent boys in the same project; their practice of intimidating businessmen into submission; and their destruction of the environment. The film sums up the current mission of many Italian mafia movies, by offering "a new gaze into the Camorra underworld, stripping away its mythology, magnifying the incongruous mannerisms of the *camorristi*, surveying with an almost anthropological gaze the total desolation of their lives, their confinement in a world without hope, without a single moment of truce or reprieve." Antonello's assessment places the entire mafia genre in perspective: in this case an Italian perspective, which could, and should, inform America's eager consumption of mobster fare. Renga's *sui generis* anthology performs much the same function. It gives readers, for the first time, a single book including various critical accounts of Italian American and Italian mafia movies in two distinct socio-historical and cultural contexts.

A LITTLE SONG, A LITTLE DANCE, A LITTLE ZITI DOWN YOUR PANTS
Tony and Tina's Wedding and Italian American Stage Comedy

When my wife and I spent 110 dollars for tickets to *Tony and Tina's Wedding*, we weren't expecting vaudeville quite, but for better or for worse, that's what we got: A little song, a little dance, a little Ziti down Tony's pants.

Italian American comic theater, it seems, has returned to its roots; or maybe it's never grown beyond them. *Tony and Tina's Wedding, Murdered by the Mob, Revenge in the Mob, The Godfather's Meshuggenah Wedding, Vinny "The Fish" Calamari's Funeral, Joey and Maria's Comedy Wedding Cruises*: These ubiquitous dinner-theater productions, the most popular form of contemporary Italian American stage comedy, bear a striking resemblance to Italian American vaudeville shows of yesteryear; which shows, by the 1960s, had all but disappeared from view, as Italian Americans made their way onto the mainstream American stage and into the mainstream American theater-going public (Aleandri, "Theater" 635; Tedesco 361-367). Over the past two decades, aside from a few productions of literate works—such as the plays of Richard Vetere, the 1999 revival of Albert Innaurato's twenty-four year-old Broadway hit "Gemini," and Frank Ingrasciotta's 2009 one-man show *Blood Type: Ragu*—campy spectacles are the only Italian American comedies on the mainstream American stage.

Early Italian American theater, particularly vaudeville, drew on the Italian American community for material, and was performed—usually in Italian dialect—for an Italian American audience. Early theater troupes established the forms that remain the stock in trade of contemporary Italian American dinner theater companies. Of the early theatrical forms, the *macchietta coloniale* and the *caffè-concerto* have exerted the greatest influence on contemporary productions.

The *macchietta coloniale* was an extended sketch, akin to the later comic monologue form, in which a character type (such as the *Cafone Furbo*, or Shrewd Boor, of master *macchiettista* Farfariello [Eduardo Migliaccio]) (Tedesco 361), usually a Southern Italian peasant type, finds himself or herself in a comically unpleasant situation, often a result of cultural and linguistic alienation in America. Like its dinner-theater descendants, such a sketch usually got a lot of comic mileage out of "Italo-Americanese" (Aleandri, "Theater" 633), malapropism and other misuses of language. Italian Americans of the era, most of whom lived outside of the American mainstream, found sources of identity and comfort in seeing and hearing Italian American character types on an American stage, even if those types parodied the immigrant's cultural ignorance and sense of alienation in the New World. Audiences received the caricatures with good humor, since, in the hands of a premier *macchiettista,* even The Great Caruso and other *prominenti* became subjects for comedy. In this context audiences could take such subjectification as a compliment (Aleandri, *Italian-American* 91).

The *macchietta* itself formed a part the *caffè-concerto*, a variety show of sorts, involving strolling musicians, chanteuses, and comedians performing in a coffee house setting, interacting with an audience of working-class Italian immigrants (75). Setting an important precedent, performers in the *caffè-concerto,* like other vaudevillians, often used established bits and songs as the bases for improvisation.

Other vaudeville of the early twentieth century also took Italian Americans as subjects of its humor, but usually as subjects for comic derision. Italian Americans most often appeared on the mainstream vaudeville stage as immigrant members of large families, often of large criminal families, but always of families who murdered the English language (Mintz 21-22). In this case, the comedy of stereotypes and malapropisms expressed the hostility and sense of superiority that many Americans felt toward the four million Italian immigrants who arrived in America during the four decades from 1880-1920 (24). This hostility and haughtiness found expression, for example, in the 1891 lynching of eleven Italian immigrants falsely accused of murdering a New Orleans police captain, as well as in the writings of leading public intellectuals such as Edward Alsworth Ross, who, writing in 1914, noted Italian immigrants' "lack of mental ability" and tendency to be "volatile, unstable, soon hot, soon cool" (qtd. in LaGumina, *WOP!* 138-39). As these and other stereotypes of Italian Americans have persisted—the loud, dumb man, the long-suffering woman—so too has the comedy of derision of Italian American characters.

Since the hey-day of vaudeville, the five best-known stage plays of Italian American life are Clifford Odets' *Golden Boy*, Arthur Miller's *A View from the Bridge* (transformed into an opera in 1999), Tennessee Williams' *The Rose Tattoo*, Joseph Bologna and Renee Taylor's *Lovers and Other Strangers*, and Innaurato's *Gemini*. Produced on the heels of an Italian American ethnic Renaissance, *Gemini* is the only play aside from Bologna and Taylor's thirty-three year-old *Lovers* that is a comedy, that is written by an Italian American, and that has enjoyed a successful mainstream theater run (at Broadway's Little Theater, from 1977 to 1981. (Those of us over a certain age may recall the equally successful television commercials, featuring the show's signature line, "Take human bites!"—spoken, atypically for this play, by a non-Italian American character.)

Although Italian American playwrights such as Mario Fratti (*Nine*), Julie Bovasso (*Gloria and Esperanza*), and Joseph Pintauro (*Snow*

Orchid and *The Raft of the Medusa*) have consistently had their plays produced off-Broadway and occasionally on Broadway, realistic comic theater involving complex Italian American characters has rarely appeared in the spotlight of the mainstream American stage. Since *Gemini*'s Broadway run a generation ago, such comedy has gone straight to the silver screen by way of John Patrick Shanley and other Italian American playwrights-turned-screenwriters[12] Even in *Gemini*, a comedy featuring demi-round, quasi-dynamic characters, Italian Americans appear on the contemporary American stage as mere types: loutish members of loud families and those martyrs who endure them.

Italian American theatrical companies like Kairos Italy Theater, La Bottega, and Teatromania are few, and most often focus on productions of Italian, not Italian American, work. Meanwhile, the mainstream theater audience has limited expectations of Italian American characters, based on predominant Italian American types in film and other media (Gambino 275-85). This atmosphere has assured that Italian American comic theater would develop from the only form in which it has ever truly existed: vaudeville. It is a form that lingers in our collective cultural consciousness through its adaptation for film and television; a form plastic enough to allow for simultaneous derision (270) and identification with its subject.

Tony and Tina's Wedding has grown from the work of a particular theatrical improvisation group, Artificial Intelligence, inheritors of the vaudeville tradition. An Italian American writer and performer,

---

[12] Shanley's 1988 play, *Italian American Reconciliation: A Folktale,* presents four realistic, if stylized, Italian American characters trying to solve the mysteries of love and marriage. It had only a brief run at the Manhattan Theatre Club's City Center Stage II. Judging from the play's unremarkable plot and maddeningly detached tone, one might conclude that Shanley owes its appearance on a mainstream stage to the popularity of *Moonstruck*, his Academy Award-winning film of the same year.

Nancy Cassaro, a member of this group, created Tony and Tina in the early 1980s (Corcoran). By 1985, she and her fellow performers had built an entire show around the stereotypical Italian American bride and groom and their enormous, loud families. The result is a combination of various *macchiette* in a *caffè-concerto* atmosphere. Entering its thirtieth year of production, having enjoyed extended runs in cities across America, this most popular of Italian American dinner-theater productions asks its audience to enjoy participating as "guests" at the wedding, while at the same time deriving pleasure from deriding the wedding's principals.

Guests arrive at the wedding venue—often an actual church—where Tony Angelo and Tina Vitale are shortly to be married in a Catholic ceremony. Upon arrival, they are greeted at the entrance and in the lobby of the church's basement by actors already in character as relatives and friends of the families. As my wife and I walked in, one middle-aged female actor in a huge bouffant wig and chintzy black dress with gold lamé embroidery, standing next to an older male actor in a rumpled dinner suit, in her heavy New York accent—stage Italian Americans usually have New York, if not Chicago, accents—asked a group of young women audience members, "You remember Uncle Louie?"; then, turning to Uncle Louie, remarked, "You remember the girls. They used to roller skate in the driveway."

Although much of the dialogue changes from performance to performance, its effect is always the same: to make audience members, often tourists from America's hinterland, feel a part of an urban, large, and boisterous Italian American *famiglia*. It is an effect that allows them to shed presumed Anglo American inhibitions and live it up *all'Italiana*. On the night we attended, the guests, who took part in the festivities and laughed loudly at Tony and Tina's stereotypically buffoonish behavior, were, generally speaking, fair-skinned and blond, and spoke with the accents of other regions, and sported pastel clothing and fanny packs. They appeared to be neither Italian Americans nor New Yorkers. The show's producer, Joseph Corcoran, confirmed that seventy-five percent of the tickets to the Broadway show's performances are sold to people residing outside of New York State.

The effect of the performance is not strictly, as Richard Gambino claims, to offer up Italian American stereotypes as subjects for ridicule (270), although, admittedly, it may be the most powerful effect. Leaving aside their response to the mediocre wedding feast, I perceived in the audience's playful dancing and banter during the performance at least a hint of positive cross-cultural identification. So what then is the outcome of giving mainstream theatergoers the chance to identify with distorted Italian American characters while serving those characters up as food for ridicule?

At one point during the church ceremony, Tina's grandmother (more recently played in the New York production by the brilliant Italian American writer and performance artist Annie Lanzillotto), like a figure from a yellowed immigrant photograph or from a film like Woody Allen's "Broadway Danny Rose," in her black shawl, hat, and veil, stood up and yelled, "We are all family." This Old Country *nonna,* the Italian-accented uncle, the brash aunt, the overbearing father of the groom, the overbearing, widowed mother of the bride, the buffoonish Tony, and the crude, gum-chewing Tina are all Italian American types, recreated *alla macchietta*. What's more, they are types by now familiar to American audiences.

In church and at the reception that follows, these types chaff the paying guests, insult and embrace each other, sing and dance, and otherwise disport themselves. In essence, they recreate the "haphazard," audience-participatory entertainment of the vaudeville stage and the *caffè-concerto* (Aleandri, *Italian American* 75, 85), all in formal (and stereotypically garish) wedding attire. The audience, for their part, can revel in joining for the evening an Italian American family, seeing the family as a comically ridiculous entity, or doing both simultaneously.

This choice is possible and appealing, because for all their movement into the American mainstream, Italian Americans have apparently not achieved complete structural assimilation (Conforti 38); that is, they have not gained complete social acceptance as mainstream Americans. By their names, and often by their customs and appearance, Italian Americans are identifiable and identified as cultural others, and occasionally still as racial others. This reality has helped perpetuate Italian American film and television stereotypes, such as those presented in any number of Mafia comedies like Jonathan Demme's *Married to the Mob* and Ivan Reitman's *Analyze This*; in romantic comedies like Nancy Savoca's *True Love* and Shanley's *Moonstruck*; in television shows like *Who's the Boss?*, *That's Life*, *Everybody Loves Raymond*, *Jersey Shore*, and various mafia family reality shows; and in television commercials for *Gemini*, restaurants like The Olive Garden, and products like Prince Spaghetti. Ironically, these productions use the genuinely Italian American *macchietta* form to present Italian Americans as vengeful grandmothers; slovenly, doting mothers; fat, ignorant fathers; brutal, stupid sons; and tough, tacky, promiscuous daughters. In its turn, the mass media presence of these stereotypes has fostered a public sense of Italian Americans' social otherness, as it has popularized contemporary, type-driven Italian American stage comedies.

Of course, like Italian American vaudeville, dinner-theater comedies, particularly *Tony and Tina's Wedding*, exhibit, along with stereotypes, some genuine Italian American cultural phenomena. Anthropologist Thomas Belmonte points out that the wedding of two Italian

Americans often brings together large, sometimes boisterous groups of people who are not afraid to show their emotions (9), groups such as the Vitales and the Angelos. We can safely say then that *Tony and Tina's Wedding* exaggerates but does not fabricate a possible Italian American nuptial experience. (I myself have attended numerous Italian American weddings and non-Italian American New York area weddings that resemble Tony and Tina's.)

The show also portrays with some accuracy the ambivalence of Italian American men toward religious ceremony. Throughout the wedding ceremony, the men of the wedding party appear as though they are trying and frequently failing to behave themselves. Shifting in their seats, wearing sunglasses, greeting each other in loud voices, and rolling their eyes at older family members and clergy, they try hard to pipe down when an overeager nun arises to lead the characters and guests in a hymn; still, as she speaks and sings, they make faces and whisper to each other, until she reprimands them, at which time, like schoolboys, they apologize. Later in the performance, Tony makes a Pope joke. This attitude reflects the reality that Italian American men, whose forbears were accustomed to a more public, pagan, mutable, and accessible brand of Catholicism, have never fully adjusted to the more ascetic, rigid, doctrinaire Irish variety that took hold in the immigrant communities of the early twentieth century (16).

At any number of Italian American weddings and other grand occasions, I have heard the type of Italian American language that the principals of *Tony and Tina's Wedding* speak. At one point during the reception, when Tony spills something on his white tuxedo, the mother of the bride calls him a *gavonn'*, Southern Italian dialect for *cafone*, a boor. Uncle Louie wishes *"tanti auguri a tutti,"* "best of luck to everyone." And even the presiding Irish priest takes the cue, urging everyone to *"mangia,"* when dinner appears.

While it makes use of stereotype and genuine ethnic totem, *Tony and Tina's Wedding* also appeals to mainstream audiences through universal, vaudevillian topical humor. A staff of writers revise the basic script periodically, and actors improvise dialogue (Corcoran). As my wife and I found our seats in church, the groom's father leaned over to us and quipped, "The family [my son]'s marrying into, they're a little wacky. It's like, 'Attention, K-Mart shoppers...'" At the reception, when the band played Madonna's 1998 hit "Ray of Light," Tina exclaimed to her new husband, "Swear to God, Ton', you're my ray of light." This just before the entire wedding party attempted the Macarena.

The production ends on an even more vaudevillian note, with a kickline of family members and catering hall staff, the subjects of various film and television-inspired *macchiette* (including the funereal Italian grandmother), hoofing their way through the nightclub classic, "New York, New York." As guests sing along, the *caffè-concerto* returns to life.

The audience, dialogue, and structure of lesser-known shows such as the widely produced *Murdered by the Mob*, also follow the vaudeville formula. *Murdered* makes a great deal, for instance, of its characters' tendency toward malapropism. One young mafioso named Vito Gucciani responds to the assassination of another mafioso by telling the audience, "I know things before they happen. It's like I'm psychotic."

Murdered requires even more audience participation than *Tony and Tina*, going so far as to award prizes for best performances by audience members. (The night I attended, perhaps inspired by the presence of my Italian American parents, I won third prize.) Written by another Italian American woman, Joan Pacie, and her Italian American spouse, Ron Pacie, the show is a more recent phenomenon than *Tony and Tina*. It began production in 1996. The night my parents and I attended, the entire audience, it seemed, sat waiting downstairs at the bar, sounding and looking to my ears and eyes thoroughly Italian American amidst the regular African American clientele. Later, as they ate and drank, sang along with Dean Martin and Louie Prima, and exchanged Italian curses with the performers, I had the sense they had all been guests at other staged Italian American weddings, and that in this parody of a ritual they were seeing not just what the non-Italian American audience was seeing, but also, in a supremely post-modern gesture of ethnicity, were recognizing symbols of their ethnic identity.

Although neither *Murdered by the Mob* nor any of the lesser Italian American dinner theater productions mentioned above has enjoyed *Tony and Tina*'s success, the kinship of these spectacles to earlier Italian American stage forms, and their profusion, make them worthy subjects for Italian American culture studies, ethnic studies, and theater studies in general. They suggest that at the very least we should discuss and not dismiss the connections between a cultural group's indigenous art forms and the sources and nature of its types and stereotypes.

Meanwhile, those of us concerned with Italian American images in the arts look forward to a more realistic brand of Italian American comic theater, one rooted in genuine experience and expressed through complex characters. We wait for the day when their playbill covers—like the one for the 1999 off-Broadway production of *Gemini*—no longer need to show a heaping portion of gravy-laden spaghetti.

Works Cited

Aleandri, Emilise. *The Italian-American Immigrant Theater of New York City*. Charleston, SC: Arcadia Publishing, 1999.

———. "Theater History." Salvatore LaGumina, et. al., eds. *The Italian American Experience: An Encyclopedia*. New York: Garland Publishing, 2000.

Belmonte, Thomas. "The Contradictions of Italian American Cultural Identity: An Anthropologist's Personal View." Ed. Pellegrino D'Acierno. *The Italian American Heritage.* New York: Garland Publishing, 1999. 3-20.

Conforti, Joseph. "Italian Americans as 'Ethnics': Description or Derogation?" Eds. Jerome Krase and Judith N. DeSena. *Italian Americans in a Multicultural Society.* StonyBrook, NY: Forum Italicum, 1994. 35-43.

Corcoran, Joseph. Personal Interview. 3 August 1999.

Gambino, Richard. "The Crisis of Italian American Identity." Eds. A. Kenneth Ciongoli and Jay Parini. *Beyond the Godfather: Italian American Writers on the Real Italian American Experience.* Hanover, NH: UP of New England, 1997. 269-288.

LaGumina, Salvatore, ed. *WOP!: A Documentary History of Anti-Italian Discrimination in America.* San Francisco: Straight Arrow Books, 1973.

Mintz, Lawrence E. "Humor and Ethnic Stereotypes in Vaudeville and Burlesque." *MELUS* 21.4 (Winter 1996): 19-28.

Pacie, Joan and Ron Pacie. Telephone Interview. 6 August 1999.

Tedesco, Jo Ann. "Sacraments: Italian American Theatrical Culture and the Dramatization of Everyday Life." Ed. Pellegrino D'Acierno. *The Italian American Heritage.* New York: Garland Publishing, 1999. 353-386.

Mario Soldati's Italian Americans[13]

In Italy Mario Soldati was a celebrity: author of forty-nine books; director of a dozen films, host of two popular 1950s television series; and best known for *America primo amore,* a book now, surprisingly, out of print. In America Soldati was little known during his lifetime, and if remembered here at all (He died in 1999), is certainly not remembered for *America primo amore* (*America, First Love*), a book all about this country, and one which has never been translated into English.

A native of Torino, Soldati had his first major publication, a play, *Pilato,* in 1924. Five years later he published a book of well-received short stories, *Salmace.* That same year, 1929, the young writer traveled to America, to New York City, to Columbia University, on a fellowship in art history, in part to escape fascist oppression. He remained in the United States for two years, returning again in 1932 and 1933. *America primo amore* comprises Soldati's impressions of American society during this period.

Pieces that would become chapters of the book appeared in *Il Lavoro,* a socialist Genovese newspaper: the first in 1930, the last in 1935. Bemporad, a Florentine house, published *America primo amore* in 1935, with cover art by Soldati's close friend, Carlo Levi; this after Bompiani had suggested politically expedient changes, which Soldati refused to make. Successive, enlarged editions appeared in 1945 and 1956, from Einaudi; in 1959, 1976 and 1990, from Mondadori; in 1992, from Rizzoli; and in 2003, from Sellerio. Soldati, his publish-

---

[13] Quotations from Soldati's text are in my translation.

ers, and his audiences kept returning to *America primo amore*, because he and they were obsessed, the way lovers are obsessed, with America.

Soldati compared the *"primo amore,"* the first love, to a first voyage, claiming that both were sicknesses, like the obsession of a young man escaping an oppressive and rebellious youth, as the young author himself was (Nigro, *"Addio"* 11-12). Soldati's love for America was the *"violento amore,"* violent love, (Soldati 26) of the immigrant who is both angered by the need to leave his old home and excited by the prospect of what he will find in his new one. Such violent love easily turns to resentment, either when the lover is disappointed or when he simply does not see himself or his culture reflected in the object of his love. Soldati puts it simply: "Any love story contains some bitterness" (20). A number of Italian intellectuals—Soldati, Elio Vittorini, Cesare Pavese, and Emilio Cecchi, to name a few—felt this way about America during the fascist era. They were attracted to America's "youthful vigor, its openness and informality" (Pells 246), but repelled by what they saw as its callow savagery and the dehumanizing effects of its industry and work ethic.

Oddly, their sentiments echo the moral tenets of the fascist regime against which they were struggling.

> "Moralism", a fundamental component of fascist education for the making of the "new Italian", condemned American society as a modern Sodom where sexual freedom, the disintegration of the family, the practice of contraception, the search for material well-being, the cult of wealth, ruthless capitalism, dehumanizing technology, urban neurosis, corrupt politics, racial discrimination and organized crime were rampant. By identifying modernity as degeneration, fascism's moralists saw Americanism as the most serious manifestation of the morbid nervousness of modern life. (Gentile 10)

A great deal of Soldati's narrative concerns itself with these American vices, as well as their disturbing tendency to distort and in some cases erase centuries of European culture.

Soldati's love/hate relationship with America animates *America primo amore*. Nearly every section, nearly every passage, crackles with powerful ambivalence, critical insight, sarcasm, and wit. On one hand Soldati is in love with Americans', and immigrants', innocent sense of freedom and boundlessness. By his reckoning, Italian immigrants, at least those at the beginning of their affair with America, resemble native-born Americans in their belief in infinite possibility, which Soldati describes as "the conviction of finding oneself before a marvelous and blessed world, a land of so much air and space" (Soldati 32). But he is skeptical of this conviction. He figures New York as the locus of the American myth, a city of skyscrapers, which he deems "more or less beautiful," but whose beauty comes from "all practical and economic origins" (44). The skyscrapers are thus both beautiful and "monstrous" (44), as the subways are both a site of great democracy, aboard which "rich and poor[…]white and black; Aryans and Jews; clean and dirty; women and men; all together" (91-92), ride inside an "everyday" trap (88). The buildings and the trains, and especially the work life of American cities are to Soldati "organized American barbarities" (92). In his eyes New York and Chicago are "ruined, filthy, sad metropolises, where millions of men live in misery and degradation" (162).

Soldati's Americans, including immigrants, live to work, instead of working to live. They are victims of the protestant work ethic, which has marginalized the joy of human company and left them with "a sadness they do not admit to themselves" (174). They are numbed not only to their own joy, but to others' pain. According to

Soldati, most Americans, unlike Europeans, cannot tolerate those who are unable or unwilling to strive for material wealth.

> An older, more civilized people, even if we work, understand the sweetness of doing nothing and are ready to excuse and to help the idle, especially if we are bound to them by friendship or blood. But Americans are still barbarians: They consider the lazy person a reprobate, and place him decidedly outside society, without regard to these sorts of ties. (126)

This hard-heartedness is the cruelty of children who "do not know themselves," who "deceive themselves" about their own nature and the nature of life (42). "In America," Soldati continues, "there isn't even a law that obliges children to take care of their elderly parents who are unable to work" (126).

In his 1908 volume *Impressioni d'America*, Giuseppe Giacosa, Puccini's primary librettist, offers a similar Italian perspective on the tendency of Americans, especially America's young, the "prodigies of mechanization" (Handlin 398), to drink immoderately and act wildly. Their aimless abandon and disregard for others, writes Giacosa, "involves a conservation of energy; it imposes a rest and suspends the intellectual activity of minds, so heavily taxed and so thoroughly fatigued by business" (397). These citizens of a strange, young nation, these "child-like spirits" (Sarfatti, qtd. in Gentile 21), are, to Giacosa and Soldati alike, victims of technology and economic progress (Gentile 21). Recalling the fascist party line, Soldati suggests that Americans could temper their distemper, the effects of technology, by learning the lessons of Italian society, of an "older, more civilized people."

Giacosa illustrates the American corruption of European culture and society in a portrait of a typical Anglo American family reading the Sunday paper, which he presents as a Faustian form of easy gratification at the cost of family communion and spiritual well-being. Soldati sketches a similar scene, translated below, involving this time an Italian American family, the Costantinos, friends of a learned, refined Italian friend. The Constantinos are the perfect example of an Italian American family in an ethnic enclave who have preserved elements of bygone southern Italian Culture in America.

> Cut off from America as from Italy, they have reproduced, crystallized, between the Hudson and Long Island, Italian mentality and society as it was in the era of their emigration.
>
> We thus find in New York preserved almost under glass, the mentality of a barber from Catania circa 1890. And in a circle of family, friends, and in-laws who live near one another in the same neighborhood, we recognize the provincial and bourgeois societies of Avellino, L'Aquila, Benevento, Potenza, etc., as they existed before the Great War.

If this aspect of their behavior renders the family quaint, it does not, however, render them irrelevant. News of success from Italian Americans like the Costantinos fired the imaginations of the fascists and many other Italians of the era (Cannistraro 110-117). Soldati gives us the patriarch of the Italian American family touting a token of this success. "Mr. Costantino, sprawled on a rocking chair, had placed on his knees that kilogram of paper that is the American Sunday edition. As I passed next to him while dancing, he called out to me and with his fingers showed me the thickness of the paper, insisting with satisfaction: 'You see, *nun tenete di chiste jurnale in Italia,*" and turning to the kids: "They haven't got a Sunday Paper over there'." The Sunday Paper, *il giornale della domenica,* is, along with skyscrapers and cheap pineapples and automobiles, the preferred topic of conversation among those who have decided to content themselves with America.

The coarse Costantinos of *America primo amore* are Soldati's satirical answer to the myth of America in Italy. To Soldati's Italian readership, they have been corrective symbols of American materialism, complacency, spiritual longing, and the degradation of age-old (Italian) culture and civilization. To an American audience they may be the same, or they may be a window onto the lives of an Italian American middle class that rose in the wake of mass immigration. Unlike so many windows of Soldati's New York, it is a window with an ample view, albeit the view of a deeply disappointed lover.

WORKS CITED

Cannistraro, Phillip V. *Blackshirts in Little Italy: Italian Americans and Fascism, 1921-1929.* West Lafayette, Indiana: Bordighera Press, 1999.

Gentile, Emilio. "Impending Modernity: Fascism and the Ambivalent Image of the United States." *The Journal of Contemporary History* 28 (1993): 7-29.

Handlin, Oscar, ed. *This Was America: True Accounts of People and Places, Manners and Customs, as Recorded by European Travellers to the Western Shore in the Eighteenth, Nineteenth and Twentieth Centuries.* Cambridge, MA: Harvard UP, 1949.

Nigro, Salvatore Silvano. *"Addio...diletta America."* America primo amore. By Soldati. Ed. Salvatore Silvano Nigro. Palermo: Sellerio editore, 2003. 7-15.

Pells, Richard. *Not Like Us.* New York: Basic Books, 1997.

Soldati, Mario. *America primo amore.* Ed. Salvatore Silvano Nigro. Palermo: Sellerio editore, 2003.

Novel *Paesans*
The Reconstruction of Italian American Male Identity in Anthony Valerio's *Conversation with Johnny* and Robert Viscusi's *Astoria*

Do we need to rehabilitate the *paesan*? What I mean is, do we need to reconstruct the public identity of the Italian American man? If we survey the great cocktail party of the American literary scene, we see the faces of many Italian American men: among the writers of fiction, Don DeLillo and Richard Russo; among the poets, W. S. DiPiero and Dana Gioia; among the scholars, Frank Lentricchia and Andrew Delbanco; even among the captains of our literary industry, Leonard Riggio, Executive Chairman of Barnes and Noble, and Steve Acunto, President of CINN Group. Watching these distinguished gentlemen operate, we feel certain that the old stereotypes of Italian American men as mafiosi, brutes, sexual predators, or idiots are behind us. But then, at the same party, we overhear Italian American intellectuals and business elites lament these stereotypes, discuss their presence in movies and television shows we all know (and in some ways admire), and we begin to wonder.

A generation ago, John Gotti, from jail, was making the cover of *Time* magazine. Much to the chagrin of Italian American critics, Spike Lee's *Jungle Fever* was exploiting the public preconception of a mythic Italian American male "penchant for violence, and sexist relations with women" (Viscusi, qtd. in Verdicchio 187); around the same time, the cast of Saturday Night Live played a running sketch in which a pair of lecherous waiters with hokey Italian accents assaulted female patrons of their restaurant (usually guest hosts of the show) with unwanted amorous attention, calling them *"Bellissima!"*, until finally forcing them into sexually compromising positions. And then, of course, we had the work of Mario Puzo, whose *The Godfather* continues to be read and seen by millions. Not to mention his late-career, best-selling novel and hit Mafia miniseries *The Last Don*, which, according to network promos for its sequel, *The Last Don II*, "captivated over fifty-two million viewers."

Wide-release films, syndicated television shows, video rentals, and cable television help to perpetuate negative Italian American stereotypes. Among the creatures of film, syndication, and video who will not die are The Fonz of "Happy Days," a macho Latin lover type, Tony Manero of *Saturday Night Fever,* a less intelligent Latin lover type, Rocky Balboa, a brute, and Puzo's cast of colorful mafiosi. In 1984, Rudolph Vecoli cited a study of the images of Italian Americans presented on television, which concluded that the public was treated to twice as many negative portrayals as positive ones, and that "one out of six [Italian American characters] was engaged in criminal activities, most held low status jobs, and the majority did not speak English correctly" (53). Although shows such as HBO's *The Sopranos* —conceived with a great deal of cultural savoir-faire by the pseudonymous Italian American David Chase—have complicated existing stereotypes, many shows and films have simply perpetuated them.

Whatever we may think of the above-mentioned characters as models for emulation, great numbers of Italian American men have found sources of identity in the stereotypes that films like *Saturday Night Fever* and *The Godfather* promulgate. Vecoli rightly claims that although some Italian-Americans responded to *The Godfather* and its sequels by protesting and picketing the films, many took them as "the Italian-American equivalent of Alex Haley's *Roots*" (55). Vecoli also recognizes that such "self-caricature and self-denigration" result from the lack of awareness of cultural material for the construction of positive Italian American identities (55). To this point in history, Italian American artists and intellectuals have not gone far enough in mining for their fellow Italian Americans the cultural marble trapped inside a mountain of negative images.

As Robert Viscusi implies, Italian Americans remain imprisoned in the ugly cinder block (jail)house constructed by Puzo, Coppola, Scorsese, and others ("Divine" 70). It is a house full of myths, mostly disparaging ones, which continue to attend Italian American manhood. Sonny Corleone is a creature who lives by brute lust and force, but we continue to grieve his gory death. Goodfella Tommy is demented, criminal, and ruthless, but we celebrate him in continual quotation of his menacing questions: "What the f--- is so funny about me? Am I here to f---in' amuse you?" And his *paesani*, his victims, however rounded they may be in some respects, remain gangsters, whose lines we also parrot. So novelist Anthony Valerio's remark on the power of Italian Americans' (or any group's) powers of self-determination tells the story of Italian Americans' complicity in America's vulgar construction of the *paesan*: "We create our own myths" (Interview with Lopate).

At this point, I feel the need to step back and ask, is the foregoing analysis part of Italian American men's continuing identification with stereotypes? Or is it part of the Italian American elite's overreaction to those stereotypes? Or is it part of a reaction in the nick of time? Is it possible that we can simply chalk up stereotypes of Italian American men to a lively American tradition of ethnic humor.[14] Or should we be truly concerned about the ramifications of these stereotypes?

---

[14] In 1996, *MELUS* dedicated an entire issue to considering, and in a few articles celebrating, this tradition.

Richard Gambino claims that "Italian American identity is in danger of being dissolved in a sea of inauthentic myths. Italian Americans shout "We are!" but an army of those who define them answers, "Look who's talking! Criminals, buffoons, racists, and *cafoni*" ("Crisis" 270). If Gambino protests too much—his own oft-cited 1974 study of Italian Americans, *Blood of My Blood*, itself stereotypes African Americans, and, in its quaint way, Italian Americans too—he can be forgiven, since he does recognize that many Italian Americans share "a preoccupation with setting the Italian American record straight" (275). This preoccupation, he argues, fosters a defensive attitude among Italian American intellectuals, a trait that in turn leads other intellectuals to dismiss their laments. And so protests like his fall on deaf ears. Perhaps, then, protest is not the way.

But what is? Gambino is on to it, I believe, when he observes that "surrealism is the most marked quality" of Italian American experience today. While they "need not love" their surreal state of being, "if they are going to understand themselves," and, I would add, understand how to present their identities to the public, they must come to terms with it (276). Like other victims of stereotyping, Italian American men particularly need to understand that they have fashioned their identities in part from an immaterial culture of semi-fictional images.

Whether Italian Americans shrug or wring they hands over their surreal dilemma, they can be sure of one thing: Italian American writers have been hard at work on a post-Puzo reconstruction of Italian American male identity for decades now. Relatively early on, this reconstruction produced two masterpieces of cultural renewal that passionately embrace, and in embracing manipulate, the surrealism of public Italian American male identity. They are Robert Viscusi's 1995 novel *Astoria* and Anthony Valerio's 1997 novel *Conversation with Johnny* (subsequently republished *Lefty and the*

Button Men (2000) and *Lefty and Her Gangsters* (2011).

These two novels recall to me, surreally, metaphorically, my hometown, oddly named Lynbrook, the name a syllabic anagram of Brooklyn, home of the nation's largest Little Italy, and the borough of New York City whence most of Lynbrook's post-War residents migrated. Many of the residents of Lynbrook are Italian American, and a great number of these are employed in construction, specifically in home improvement. Those Italian American men of Lynbrook who improve homes tend to specialize in one of two sub-fields: renovation or remodeling. The renovator takes the existing structure of a room and restores it to a state of apparent newness, while the remodeler demolishes what have to that point been the room's immutable features and replaces them with borrowings from cultures and decorating magazines far removed from the organic post-War, suburban vernacular of Lynbrook. They belong to two distinct schools of artistic endeavor, the renovator and remodeler, yet they share some methods, the remodeler occasionally refurbishing and the renovator occasionally demolishing.

Anthony Valerio, from one part of Long Island, is a renovator; Robert Viscusi, from another part of Long Island, is a remodeler. Both authors work to recreate the gaudy, mysterious, enigmatic space that is public Italian American male identity. *Astoria* and *Conversation with Johnny* are their open houses.

But why stick to just one metaphor when dealing with a subject so surreal as Italian American maleness?

Imagine for a moment that the flesh and bone of Viscusi's remodeled Italian American man is language, in the most literal sense. Imagine this, because *Astoria* is a book that demands we consider its narrator not as character in a singular representative drama of Italian American values, heritage, and spirit, but, foremost, as a speaking subject. His identity remains as mutable as language, because "any pretence of stable masks" in such a drama "is likely to be premature, given the situation" of Italian Americans (163). By which I take him to mean that Italian Americans, like African Americans and other groups who often express a strong sense of difference from mainstream American society, are still in the process of reconstructing their collective public identity from the residue of history, memory, and the failure of both (what Viscusi's narrator calls *l'Astoria*—the Italian American neighborhood of his youth, the Italian word for "ahistory," and a pun on the Italian word for "history"). Then, too, Viscusi's novel recognizes that only rarely has the Italian American man been publicly figured or publicly perceived as a creature of words, a voice, a person who knows and will freely share his knowledge, his aporiae, and his anxiety about both.

Instead, the public Italian American man we know is Martin Scorsese and Nicholas Pileggi writing Jimmy Conway speaking through Robert DeNiro telling Henry Hill, "You learned the two most important lessons in life: Always keep your mouth shut, and never rat on your friends." Important lessons for a mafioso, someone bound by *omertà*, the traditional Italian code of silence and honor—just ask the ghost of John Gotti—but not necessarily for others. Still, Italian Americans and others translate Scorsese's and Pileggi's characters not as ridiculous, but as praiseworthy men. After seeing "Goodfellas," a one-time student of mine told me with a gleam in his eye and a chuckle that DeNiro, the son of a well-regarded abstract expressionist painter, had to be a gangster in real life. Generally speaking, when America has considered Italian American men *qua* Italian American men, it has been this way, lightly, as reflections of the don or the amoral lover, and not as Viscusi's weighty and witty scholar.

In *Astoria*, his speaker, this scholar, the narrator/hero, speaks a path away from the mute and simple polar stereotypes of the Godfather and the hot-blooded lover (Scapp, "Watermelons" 34, 37). Viscusi's bipolar I/He is anything but mute and simple. As he himself suggests, he is a consciousness in constant intellectual, sensory motion (311), speaking a path directly toward a model of identity as volubility, as voice: Napoleon. In the narrator's mind, Napoleon answered "the salvoes" of those who hailed him as "the very opposite of what he wished to become" "with each time some new exuberance of discipline and labor depositing his signature, in the end, upon the historian's page" (155-56). Napoleon's acts, figured as verbal here, consume the "boundaries" of being and make him a model of verbal Reconstruction. *Astoria* is in this way a genealogy and archaeology of male identity, through a man who unintentionally fostered the unification of the Italian homeland.[15]

"*Qu'est-ce que c'est la propriété?*" What is ownership (implying self-ownership)? Viscusi's narrator asks. "Answer: *La propriété, c'est le vol*": "*Vol*," the French word meaning "flight" and "theft," and connoting the English "volume." In flying across time and space from Astoria to Paris, he embarks on a voluble "war against silence" (142), against the code of *omertà*, his own family's silence on the past, which obscures Italian heritage and with it essential components of an intelligible, comfortable Italian American identity. His is flight born of frustration, because in Astoria the signs of heritage show themselves but defy reading; so he must appropriate these signs and alter their significance. In America, the narrator tells us, "the more we" [Italian Ameri-

---

[15] Napoleon's Italian administration, designed to discourage notions of Italian unity and Italian identity, ultimately had the opposite effect, encouraging cooperation among ruling interests in Italy, spawning the creation of secret Italian societies that helped to train future Italian patriots. For a more complete account of Napoleon's influence on Italian unity and identity, see Spencer Di Scala's *Italy: From Revolution to Republic*, 20-34.

cans] "became a part of the landscape the more we were visible against it as objects of a high color and an assignable price" (154). This dilemma causes frustration and duplicity which compels, impels, propels him from an Astoria of the past, to an Italy of the future, through a Paris of past, present, and future, via Napoleon and his mother.

When, in "A Note from the Author," Viscusi claims that *Astoria* "is a woman's book written by a man" (7), he means that the credit for his narrator's identity as an Italian American man goes to the narrator's mother. She recalls to him all the "Bourbon floridity" (105) of the Italian American *nouveau riche*, his first community, whose embrace he had failed to escape through an American education (and an education in Americanness) which "had been a way of putting distance between ourselves [young Italian Americans of his generation] and this continuous explosion of ormolu and mirrors" (105) which he had always understood as Italianness. Upon her death, "the dying mother," he tells us, "said to him now you are entirely born" (95). Any sense of identity must come, after all, in one way or another, from the Italian mother. She is for him the pith of *Astoria* and its various puns in the novel, meaning *la storia*, the real history of his family, *l'astoria*, the ahistory of silence about that history, and *Astoria*, the formerly Italian American neighborhood in Queens.[16] All the while his consciousness travels, it remains forever attached but also free of the old neighborhood and *ancien* Italian American *régime*.

The structure of the novel itself speaks to the narrator's mother. She is the last of "The Invalids," the title of the first section and the name of the edifice housing Napoleon's tomb, through which the narrator realizes the connection between Napoleon and his mother,

---

[16] Viscusi first intended to call his novel *L'Astoria*, but called it *Astoria* instead, to avoid confusion with Jerre Mangione's and Ben Morreale's history of Italian Americans, *La Storia*, published in 1992.

the connection between them and his Italianness. His realization is the germ of "The Terror," the title of the second section, the name of the radical revolutionary period that opened the door to Napoleon's reign, and the name for the sense of dislocation that the narrator, like his mother, experiences. It is only in "The Revolution," the final section of the novel, that the narrator gains his freedom from both the Invalids and the Terror, and only because his mother sets him free. Her final act is essential, because, as the narrator claims, it allows an Italian American slave to ignorance, like a pre-Revolution French peasant, to become an Italian American man "free to go" if he likes, wherever his mind and words lead him (303)—at least in theory and utterance.

This freedom, his reconstructed identity (represented by the pronoun "I"), ultimately consists of reading himself (represented by the pronoun "he") in search of knowledge and in the act of publishing that knowledge in a scholarly prose as distant from stereotypical guinea "dems" and "doses" as it can be. In Viscusi's *Astoria*, the Italian American "I" is

> a telephone book full of dirty pictures, a crunching of deep plates that supports, among other its epiphenomena, Paris, l'Astoria, Sunnyside, Rome, a bottle full of green jelly beans and little marshmallows, a dead buck strapped across the fender of my uncle's 1956 Chevy, opening wide the double doors of the Amphithéâtre Richelieu to the assumption of the Chair in the History of the French Revolution by a quintet of entertainers chosen at random one Friday night in Les Halles, a juggler, a gymnast, the fellow with the Hurdy-Gurdy who sings like Aznavour, the Living Mannequin, and of course, the Storyteller with the Yellow Buttons...." (184)

In other words, the narrator's new identity is a metaphorical construction of disparate pronouns and pieces of I/he's world, a remodeling of the Italian American man as virtuoso language.

Anthony Valerio, too, renews Italian American male identity, but unlike Viscusi, he concentrates not on remodeling but on renovating existing structures, stereotypes such as the sexual predator and the beneficent (to those who obey him) Godfather. In doing so, he conveys a communal sense of the sensitivity of Italian American *paesans*.

Conversation with Johnny, Valerio's third book of fiction, transfigures stereotypical Italian American men by making them the subject of a mock-Socratic dialogue between two such men: Johnny, the Italian American Don, and Nicholas, the Italian American lover—also the narrator—who identifies himself as a lover, with this qualification: "By lover I don't necessarily mean a big man with the ladies, I mean the way I view everything" (128). Nicholas is a successful writer who has left the old neighborhood, the Brooklyn enclave of his Italian American origin, for a life in Manhattan and beyond; he is an artist in search of beauty. According to Valerio, Nicholas is also, regarding his links to Italian American culture and society, "at the end of the line. Not only is he allergic to wheat" and therefore pasta—a symbol of Italian American cultural sustenance—"he's also having an affair with a Jewish young lady" (a cultural and religious other), and he's living in Manhattan, a world away from Bensonhurst, the ultimate Little Italy (Valerio, Interview with Lopate). One day, Nicholas, lonely and alienated from the society in which he lives, decides to go home again and meet with the local don (Valerio, Interview). During their meeting, Nicholas pleads, "Now I want the truth—what went wrong, Johnny, what went wrong with me?" (Valerio, *Conversation* 16). This is a supplicant sit-down of the kind *The Godfather* made famous, except that here the don is cultural therapist/confessor rather than benefactor or powerbroker. This twist is one way Valerio succeeds in his attempt to "humanize the don"

(Valerio, Interview), having him sit and listen as Nicholas begs him, "Help me to change, Johnny. Help me to change from a lover to an ordinary man" (128).

Subsequent artistic attempts at humanizing the don include *Analyze This* and *The Sopranos*. Both of these productions feature don characters in therapy. Valerio's use of the therapy device, however, is unique and visionary. It not only predates these films, but also shows the don in control, as therapist, not patient. This configuration emphasizes the power of Italian American culture to nurture individual identity. Johnny, the don, serves as cultural nursemaid to the reborn Italian American, Nicholas.

During their first session, Nicholas tells Johnny that he has returned on a whim of essential connection. "'I saw your eyes on the cover of *The New York Times Magazine*... I knew they could see into everything, even into my subconscious, and they cleansed it of its penchant for debunking my own, for creating the beautiful lie. Rather than the stereotype, I opted for the beautiful lie" (16). But the "beautiful lie" for which Nicholas has opted is actually another Italian American male stereotype. Having eschewed the role of don, he has chosen instead that of gigolo.[17] Fortunately, Nicholas discovers that he is too sensitive for this predatory part.

These are Valerio's novel images of Italian American men: the cultivated, vulnerable lover and the compassionate don. Their conversation, in both form and substance, dismantles stereotypes and explores undiscovered Italian American territories. Throughout the narrative, Nicholas plays Socrates to Johhny's Glaucon, responding to the latter's unreported questions with digressions on his life as lover,

---

[17] Valerio admits in his interview with Leonard Lopate, "I felt, as I was creating [*Conversation with Johnny*], that I have the potential for both [don and sensitive lover/artist], as I think maybe many Italian Americans would feel."

writer, Italian American. By reinventing this classical model of virtuous reason, Valerio counters the myth of Italian "hot-bloodedness" (Scapp 37). In response to Johnny's quiet prompts, Nicholas uses reason to parse the emotion, passion, and action of his and Johnny's experience as Italian American men.

He begins by revising the stereotypes of Italian American men inscribed in *The Godfather*—a book that Nicholas mentions several times. The first of these stereotypes is the sexual predator, embodied in Sonny Corleone, who is "so generously endowed by nature that his martyred wife feared the marriage bed as unbelievers had once feared the rack" (15). The folkloric language of the passage presents Sonny literally as well as figuratively larger-than-life. It also reveals that like most of the women characters in Puzo's novel, Sandra Corleone suffers for a Corleone man: in this case, for Sonny's sexual satisfaction. Lucy Mancini, the lover whom Sonny shoots through with the "savage arrows of his lightning-like thrusts; innumerable; torturing" (28), likewise suffers; though her suffering is not so much physical pain from Sonny's thrusts, as indignity and rejection in sexual dealings with men other than Sonny. Her own generous genital endowment, of the sort that makes Sonny legend, bars relations with normal-sized men, inspires their scorn, and obliges her to seek Sonny out. Sonny's genitals are her only sexual consolation, which she loses, along with Sonny, when he is gunned down in a Long Island suburb. In this sense, like Sonny's wife, she is, with him and without him, Sonny's sexual prey.

Valerio turns this relationship on its head in *Conversation*. Nicholas, "the lover," instead of preying upon his lover, becomes her prey. Lefty uses Nicholas as an orgasm machine and tortures him with talk of marriage, although she herself is married and never promises to get divorced. While admitting he would marry her, Nicholas struggles to keep up with her sexual demands. During one conversation with Johnny, he confesses that after one particularly strenuous sexual en-counter, he found himself "totally spent, ricotta through and through" (22). Here Valerio only hints at a vulnerability he fully explores in a later chapter entitled "The Paramour." After failing to perform in bed, Nicholas learns from the doctor that his problem is psychosomatic. The treatment? A virility pill upon whose Hellenic name Nicholas constructs a comedy of sexual dysfunction. "Xanax, the Sicilian champion come to fight for the Greeks, steps out from the ranks, and with a booming voice heard all around the countryside calls out the Trojan champion.... "Stressimpotence! Stressimpotence! Let's you and me settle this dispute with hand-to-hand combat. Winner take all!" (43).

Nicholas winds up winning the battle but losing the war. Lefty leaves him, calling him after their breakup to ask if she can include in her novel a death scene of their relationship, a scene that he himself has conjured. In this way, he becomes her literary as well as sexual prey, and Valerio not so much explodes the gigolo stereotype as transposes it. Now, the Italian American "male who is already sensitive" can find himself not only "the Latin lover (seducer) of women" (Scapp 37), but also the victim of seduction and betrayal.

Valerio renovates the stereotype of Italian American man as criminal brute through similar means. According to the stereotype, Johnny, the don, should whack those who don't accept the offers they can't refuse. Valerio takes the expectation and threat of such extreme violence, and carries it to absurd moderation. In *The Godfather, Part II*, Michael Corleone sends his lieutenant and even his own brother out for rides from which they never return. In the chapter "Lesson on Paradise Island," Nicholas suggests that Johnny take a similar ride with an Italian American intellectual whose father was murdered, who disrespects his wife, who invents a gangster past, and who generally does his best to live up to stereotypes of Italian American male brutality and buffoonery. Johnny will take a little ride to rehabilitate, not to brutally punish, his quarry, who is, after all, a fellow Italian American. As Nicholas imagines the scene: Johnny's voice will sound not ominous, deadly, in that order, but "ominous, sweet." He will not teach an Italian lesson by making an example of his victim, but teach a lesson in Italian Americanness by unmaking the victim of an American stereotype. He speaks against, not to, macho gangster posturing; for emotional honesty and balance; and against stereotypical hot-headed, hot-blooded "'sexist relations with women'" (Viscusi, qtd. in Verdicchio 187).

In one of the novel's final chapters, Valerio continues renovating the don image, by introducing the surreal Don Pippo, a composite of Nicholas and Johnny. Suggestive of the power of Italian American artistry and culture to transform identity (of the don, of the lover, and of all Italian American men), Don Pippo begins his narrative existence as a character in one of Nicholas's short stories. Later, he comes to life, his soul symbolically rising from Johnny, inhabiting Nicholas's place (literally his apartment), and dying. In dying, he frees Nicholas from the limited cultural memory and the sub-cultural isolation of his old Italian American neighborhood, which to that point is all the lost writer knows and all he writes of Italian America (Hack 4). Nicholas is free to forge an identity that includes the old neighborhood but is not circumscribed by it.

Don Pippo, in announcing his own demise, invokes a vision to which Nicholas and other Italian Americans might aspire.

> I am Pippo Napoli-Sicilia and I am the last of the great Dons, the last Godfather. After me, after I join Dante in the empyrean, my family of thirty million or so will not need crime to get on, because in their dark souls and untrustful minds I have placed love and

> beauty and imagination and understanding. Their olive faces will be raised to the Crystalline Heaven. They will be at the point of assimilation into the American race, prepared to ponder the American Revolution and George Washington and Thomas Jefferson and Alexander Hamilton. They will look into one another's eyes and, instead of sensing alarm, will see brother and sister in Faith, Hope and Charity. (108)

Don Pippo's vision, it turns out, is life beyond the Italian American enclave, a life that Nicholas has attempted to lead; it is a life, nonetheless, connected with other members of the Italian American community in brother and sisterhood, "Faith, Hope, and Charity," and not in a shame of olive skin or in a sense of antagonistic difference from the rest of American society; it is a life allowing for assimilation as well as ethnicity, for "Yang the Japanese shoemaker and Bella the female butcher and Juan the Spanish fish vendor and Jake the Jewish pizza maker... Samir, the gay Palestinian restaurateur, and Gari, the albino Russian musician" (110-11) joined in society with Nicholas, the Italian writer.

As is apparent in this passage, Valerio's fiction concerns itself with Italian American male identity bound not only to the actions and images of Italian American men in isolation, but also to their interactions with Americans of other races and ethnic heritages, and especially to their interactions with women. The final passage of *Conversation* intimates that, for men, women—like Odysseus's Penelope and Dante's Beatrice—often symbolize fulfillment. In this passage, Nicholas, speaking to a gathering of the Dante Society of Westchester (at which he meets Lefty, his secular Beatrice [Hack 4]), tells the story of "the first Italian patriot, Silvio Pellico" (145). Imprisoned in a Venetian dungeon, Pellico, upon seeing women prisoners in a courtyard, exclaims, "'Woman is for me a creature so admirable, so sublime, the mere seeing, hearing and speaking to her enriches my mind with such...'" (146). The ellipses imply Valerio's ambivalence toward Pellico's vision of women. His male characters may expect fulfillment in them, but should they? And will they find it?

Critic Ed Hack makes a point worth noting: Just as "Aristophanes insists" in Plato's *Symposium* that "Human sexual attraction," the mutual desire for male/female union is really the desire to recapture an original "wholeness of personality," so Nicholas believes that he will be made whole in his union with a woman, namely Lefty (2). At one point in the novel, in fact, he envies Johnny his marriage. "Wherever you go," Nicholas tells the don, "your wife and mother make you whole" (*Conversation* 71). Later, Nicholas declares, "I want to go home, Johnny. That is, I want to make a home with the woman I love. My home doesn't have to be in Brooklyn or Queens or on Staten Island. It could be anywhere on the face of the earth, and I'll buy nice things and learn to care for them. Cook and in my garden grow broccoli-rappe"—broccoli-rappe, which earlier in the novel is a symbol of Nicholas's romantic fulfillment—"Despite my age"—around forty-five—"I'm even thinking of having children. Tell me what to do" (30). Johnny answers with a job offer, not a viable solution to Nicholas's romantic dilemma. Nicholas acknowledges that the job, as maître d' of a Brooklyn restaurant, would lead him to romance "the widows" (30), women too old and sad to fulfill him. The rest of the novel's romantic plot, Lefty's departure from his life, implies further that Nicholas may have to settle for memories of interaction with women as building blocks of his identity.

For Valerio's Italian American men, fulfillment means an Italian American identity free of conflicts between Italian custom and American aspiration. Their desire for women to help create that identity may stem from Plato as well as from "the original loss of [Italian

American] Mama" (5).[18] Or it simply may echo Dante and John Fante in presenting us with the continually disappointed male hope that women will solve the conflicts of time, of space, of society, of ethnicity, by simply loving men.

Valerio, like Viscusi, presents us, finally, with men who define themselves in relation to women and who define themselves on the page; in doing so, he mediates between Italian American subject and American audience. Of his first encounter with Johnny, Nicholas explains, "Our first shared look is hard, wildly physical, at the level of the *coglioni* [testicles]—this is how Italian men know they are men. Light from our hearts shines up to our eyes when we are with our mothers and our children, and sometimes, after giving them a hard time, our women" (*Conversation* 14-15). It is notable that Nicholas refers to "Italian" and not "Italian American" men in this passage. By emphasizing Italianness, he emphasizes ethnic difference. He and Johnny are American, but they are also, at some essential level, Italian, and as such their actions require translation for an American audience.

Viscusi's and Valerio's approaches to rehabilitating the *paesan*, reconstructing Italian American male identity, are radical, surreal, but perhaps no more so than the approaches the Italian American men of Lynbrook take to their community's houses. Theirs is a reconstruction by inhabitance, a turning of the inside out to the world, revealing previously hidden beauty and truth. In reconstructed dreams of lost Italian villas and cottages or the brick-front houses of their old Brooklyn neighborhoods, the men of Lynbrook show us their inner selves. Valerio and Viscusi likewise show us their work-in-progress, and ours: the public identity of Italian American men.

---

[18] At least one other late twentieth-century novel, Oscar Hijuelos's *The Mambo Kings Play Songs of Love* (1989), suggests that the loss of another Latin Mama, Cuban Mama, defines the Latin lover's identity.

Works Cited

Di Scala, Spencer M. *Italy: From Revolution to Republic.* Boulder, CO: Westview Press, 1995.

De Marco Torgovnik, Marianna. *Crossing Ocean Parkway.* Chicago: U of Chicago P, 1994.

Gambino, Richard. "The Crisis of Italian American Identity." *Beyond the Godfather: Italian American Writers on the Real Italian American Experience.* Eds. A Kenneth Ciongoli and Jay Parini. Hanover, N. H.: U of New England P, 1997. 269-88.

Goodfellas. Dir. Martin Scorsese. Perf. Joe Pesci, Robert De Niro, Ray Liotta, and Lorraine Bracco. Warner Brothers. 1990.

Hack, Edward. Unpublished essay, 1998.

Hijuelos, Oscar. *The Mambo Kings Play Songs of Love.* New York: Harper & Row, Publishers, 1989.

Mangione, Jerre, and Ben Morreale. *La Storia: Five Centuries of the Italian American Experience.* New York: HarperCollins, 1992.

Puzo, Mario. *The Godfather.* New York: G. P. Putnam's Sons, 1969.

Scapp, Ron. "Watermelons, Tee Shirts and Giorgio Armani: Eight-and-a-Half Epigrams on Italian-American Culture." in Scapp and Tamburri. 33-44.

Scapp, Ron and Anthony Julian Tamburri, eds. *Differentia.* 6-7 (Summer/Autumn 1994).

Valerio, Anthony. *Conversation with Johnny.* Toronto: Guernica Editions, 1997.

———. Interview with Leonard Lopate. *New York and Company.* Natl. Public Radio. WNYC, New York. 7 August 1997.

———. *Lefty and the Button Men.* Bloomington, IN: XLibris Books, 2000.

———. *Lefty and Her Gangsters.* Middletown, CT: Daisy H Productions, 2011. Kindle File.

Vecoli, Rudolph J. "The Search for an Italian American Identity." *Rivista di studi anglo-americani* 3 (1984): 29-65.

Verdicchio, Pasquale. "Spike Lee's Guineas." in Scapp and Tamburri. 177-92.

Viscusi, Robert. *Astoria.* Toronto: Guernica Editions, 1995.

———. "Divine Comedy Blues." *Beyond the Margin: Readings in Italian Americana.* Eds. Paolo A. Giordano and Anthony Julian Tamburri. Teaneck, N. J.: Fairleigh Dickinson UP, 1998. 69-79.

Anthony Valerio
The Metaphysics of Frank Sinatra

It's a warm April night. Frank Sinatra is dying. Anthony Valerio and I are strolling Greenwich Village, I turn to Anthony and ask, "Can you believe he's eighty-something?"

"What?" Valerio answers, making the arms out, palms up Italian gesture for "c'mon," "I'm the only one who gets older?"

Again, I'm the straight man, inevitable in the company of an irrepressible comedian like Valerio. To spend a half-hour in the author's company is to understand this. He walks with, to borrow his term, "a musical gait," arms akimbo, flounces of a white opera scarf dancing over his shoulder, fiery blue eyes scanning the horizon from under a black Stetson. THE ARTIST eternal in milennial Manhattan.

Valerio the man is all good humor, but Valerio the author is, to borrow more of his words, "only half an elf," comedy his tool for plumbing the sadness, irony, mystery of human experience. Like the experience of Pietro LaClacca, an ancient Italian immigrant haunting the author's Bensonhurst, his Italian American homeland. In 1986's *Valentino and the Great Italians*, "little Anthony boy," the protagonist as child, bicycling around the block, meets Mr. LaClacca. Mr. LaClacca wants to talk, but only repeats, "Hi there, little Anthony boy!" A comic situation that reveals the old man's sadness.

> He blocked the sidewalk really and truly just to talk to a little boy, the little boy who lived on the corner who hadn't as yet heard that many big people talk, so he wouldn't mind the strange accent. He might also understand that his old neighbor with the white hair

and eager face was lonely, his heart was in the country of his native language, and that in America he had used his hands instead of his mouth. He said only, "Hi there, little Anthony boy!" because he didn't know anything else to say.

Valerio's experience began on May 13th, 1940, in Bensonhurst, a section of Brooklyn where Italian Americans constructed a simulacrum of Italy: Italian cafès, Italian bakeries, Italian groceries, Italianate brick houses, and shrines to the Madonna and a panoply of saints. The author passed his formative years in this world by the shore, awash in a sea of family mythology, colorful personalities, and Italian American culture.

Always the cut-up, Valerio was expelled from several high schools, before graduating in 1958 and enrolling at Columbia College. During his college years, he discovered writers such as Gogol and Proust, his early influences. After graduating in 1962 with a B.A. in French literature, Valerio left New York for Bologna. He spent some of the next three years studying medicine, but more time wandering Italy and Spain, and writing.

Returning to America in 1965, Valerio sought a career compatible with the writer's life. He entered publishing and within a few years had become a successful editor, while cultivating an original narrative voice—sometimes waking up at three a.m. to write before work. In 1972, Valerio left publishing to teach creative writing at New York University and elsewhere. Since the early 1980s, however, Valerio has devoted most of his time to writing.

Although he claims, "I had no desire to publish at that point," and does not measure literary success by publication or financial reward, Valerio admits that his "big break" came in 1977, when *The Paris Review* published his story "The Skyjacker." It is a story told from the point of view of an Italian American soldier who hijacks a commercial flight from California and forces the pilot to land in Rome. Valerio wrote the story in order to find out "what the soldier" (whose return to Italy is an important precursor to the cultural exploration of his later fiction) "was thinking."

This early success led, in 1982, to the publication of a book of fiction (neither short story collection, nor novel, nor memoir), *The Mediterranean Runs Through Brooklyn*. A piece about Rudolph Valentino from *Mediterranean* grew into the centerpiece of Valerio's most ambitious work, *Valentino and the Great Italians*, "a weave between history and personal history," which connects the life of a narrator much like Valerio himself with those of numerous notable Italians and Italian Americans.

Although Valerio felt "called" by the Italian American community to write such a book, to fill "a gap in the culture," *Valentino* required him to betray family and ethnic group secrets. Luckily, the Italian code of silence did not prevent him from producing the most imaginative reconstruction and intimate interrogation of Italian American life yet written.

In the wake of *Valentino* came the pastiche biography of another great Italian American, *Bart: A Life of A. Bartlett Giamatti, by Him and about Him* (1991), and the impressionistic, confessional novel, *Conversation with Johnny* (1997) (subsequently re-titled *Lefty and the Button Men* and then *Lefty and Her Gangsters*).[19]

Anthony Valerio is a major Italian American fiction writer, and one of the great literary humorists our culture has produced. He

---

[19] Since the original publication of this essay in 1998, Valerio has published four more books: *Anita Garibaldi, A Biography* (2000), *The Little Sailor* (2006), *Toni Cade Bambara's One Sicilian Night* (2007, 2011), and *John Dante's Inferno: A Playboy's Life* (2012).

writes as the narrator of *Conversation* talks: "the way Frank Sinatra sings," from a sense of tragedy and comedy that transcends time and culture. In person and in his work, Valerio continues to infuse myths like Sinatra's with everlasting humanity.

Anthony Valerio's *Anita Garibaldi, A Biography*

Anita Garibaldi appeared to me one hundred and forty-five years after her death at Cesanatico, Italy, in the pages of Anthony Valerio's delightful and profound collection of stories, *Valentino and the Great Italians*. The narrator of *Valentino* gushes, "How wonderful it is for a man to have a woman fight beside him the way Anita Riberas fought side by side with Garibaldi! They were married on deck facing the setting sun and spent their honeymoon waging amphibious warfare…during Anita's first sea battle she was knocked down by a cannonball onto the bodies of three dead men. Garibaldi rushed to her. "I'm all right, I'm all right," she assured him. Her experience, like her husband Giuseppe's, speaks volumes about the humility and compassion of true greatness.

Although seldom celebrated in the United States, Anita Garibaldi has long been an icon in both South America and Italy. Born in 1821, she lived in the age of Victor Hugo, an era whose spirit lingers in the prose of romance novels. In every sense, her story is impossibly romantic, revolving as it does around a boundless love, and around crossing the boundaries of nation and continent. It is one of the first truly global epics of the modern age, done English-language justice for the first time in Valerio's new biography, *Anita Garibaldi* (Praeger, 2000). (The only other English-language account of Anita's life is Dorothy Bryant's forced, tedious 1993 novel *Anita, Anita*.)

In Valerio's account, Anita and her Peppino, as she called Giuseppe Garibaldi, professional revolutionary and liberator of Italy, join together as two halves of a cosmically fated whole. In 1839, living in

Brazil, in exile from his native Nice, Giuseppe spots his future wife from the deck of his ship. He rushes to shore, and upon meeting her face to face, exclaims, "You must be mine!" At moments like these, and there are many in the book's 170 pages, Valerio's language rises to the divine occasion. From Giuseppe's perspective he writes, "[L]ightning flashed and in the sheer, scalding light they shared the presentiment they'd met before; sought in one another's face something that made it easier to recall the forgotten past and found it, a kind of miracle, at the same time giving birth to romantic love and sibling connection...."

Anita inspires and leads Giuseppe on his fateful adventures from the shores of Brazil to the rivers and rugged terrain of Uruguay, across the Atlantic, in spirit through the Italian North, into Rome, and finally, across the mountains and across time, to their destiny. Against a backdrop of war, revolution, and the romance of modern-age political idealism, Anita lives the life of a woman who, as one of Garibaldi's comrades remarked, was "an amalgam of two elemental forces... the strength and courage of a man and the charm and tenderness of a woman, manifested by the daring and vigor with which she had brandished her sword and the beautiful oval of her face that trimmed the softness of her extraordinary eyes." She could be all woman, all warrior, all legend, all at once: New-World Beatrice, Madonna of the Pampas, mother of Italy's modern republic, people's link to the glory of Garibaldi, multicultural ideal and global celebrity. She is as remarkable as any woman in history or romantic fiction, and her tragedy is not so much her death as her absence for so long from North American view.

A conventional biographer would likely fail to revive Anita, to bring her to literary life. Illiterate, she left a few dictated notes and very little other written testimony to her experience. And while

Giuseppe describes her at length in his autobiography, he does so at several decades' distance. Historically speaking, she is a shadow that Valerio pursues through the caves of time. A preface by Philip V. Cannistraro fills in some historical blanks, while Valerio, author of one other biography, the pastiche volume *Bart: The Life of A. Bartlett Giamatti,* and heretofore mainly a writer of fiction, draws upon years of research to interpolate characters and present an American audience with a fully realized Anita.

Had she lived, the lovely South American warrior would likely have come to the United States as an immigrant. By treaty with the powers of the Austrian Empire, we learn, "General Garibaldi and his wife were to be granted safe passage through Austrian lines to a port where they were to take ship to the United States." (After the failure of his first Italian campaign, Giuseppe did indeed emigrate to Staten Island, where he lived with Antonio Meucci, inventor of the telephone.) In heroic character to the end, they refused the deal, ensuring a tragic end to Anita's "short, glorious life," and leaving us to wonder what role Anita might have played in the American women's movement of the 1840s and 1850s.

Reflecting its subject, Valerio's biography fuses epic and melodrama. Garibaldi's ship is not just a ship, but "the *Itaparica* of seven guns." And in the wake of a defeat at sea, we see the heroes in their time of trial. "She and José stood on the beach at the foot of the wooded ridge, surrounded by the wounded, horses, munitions and baggage. The wood of the ships burned; smoke thick, black and acrid with burning flesh." Bardic, Valerio sings the song of Anita's and Giuseppe's woes and triumphs, creating memorable refrains along the way. Early in life, Anita overcomes the ignominy of her status as fatherless daughter and husbandless wife, the reality that, as Valerio phrases it, "a girl without a father was like a gaucho without his horse, nothing… a wife without children was like a gaucho without his horse, nothing."

Anita Garibaldi presents a gallery of larger-than-life historical characters obscure and famous, like the "boy-officer" Emilio Morosini, the American writer Margaret Fuller, and Giuseppe himself. Anita and her husband sweep gloriously into and out of occupied Rome. "Her black feathers rose from the swaying crowd. Citizens rushed her and Peppino from all sides. Slowly, with difficulty, they reached the Egyptian obelisk in the middle of the piazza and turned their horses…Garibaldi signaled with his hands. He signaled a second time, then a dead silence came over the square." Passages such as these elevate history to myth, yet are tempered by the humanizing details of people's history. As she wanders the neighborhood of Garibaldi's youth, Anita lovingly notes, "The house was in an alley without name or number—locals called the alley *choù di buoù*, 'tail of the ox'…. She greeted the ancient quarter where Carnival had been. Huge floats decorated with cut lowers had paraded through the narrow streets." Earlier in the narrative, we learn a great deal also of the lives of nineteenth-century Brazilian peasants, hearing voices usually silent in the histories of great men and women. Valerio's combination of myth and psychological realism render Anita the most accessible of heroines. Above all, it is her consciousness that powers this account.

The Giuseppe Garibaldi of history is in this narrative a creature of Anita's world, his story entirely hers. Years after Anita's death, we learn, Giuseppe rides down from the hills to rendezvous with Victor Emanuel II, King of a newly unified Italy, "followed by a few officers and regiment of Red Shirts, the shirts dusty and stain with blood. Garibaldi wore his gray poncho, porkpie hat…Under his hat he'd tied [Anita's] colorful kerchief." Like Giuseppe's simple gesture, Valerio's biography salutes the legend that Anita Garibaldi has elsewhere and may here too someday become.

ANTHONY VALERIO'S *THE LITTLE SAILOR*
Quintessence of an *Oeuvre*

In the late 1990s and early 2000s, Anthony Valerio led a vanguard of serious authors re-releasing their novels through Web-based publishing services. Throughout his career, in fact, this most daring of Italian American writers has defied traditional genres and methods of publication. His novels—*The Mediterranean Runs Through Brooklyn* (H. B. Davis, 1982; Xlibris, 1998), *Valentino and the Great Italians, According to Anthony Valerio* (Harcourt Brace, 1986; Guernica, 1994) and *Lefty and the Button Men* (Xlibris, 1998), originally published as *Conversation with Johnny* (Guernica, 1997)—like poems, turn on imagery and cadence, and broaden the definition of "novel." His two biographies—*Bart: A Life of A. Bartlett Giamatti by Him and About Him* (Harcourt Brace Jovanovich, 1991) and *Anita Garibaldi: A Biography* (Praeger, 2001)—are just as unconventional. The first reassembles a life through quotations, commentaries, photographs and sketches; the second employs the techniques of fiction to recreate the subject through her scarce historical record. Since the last of these books appeared, Valerio has worked intermittently and collaboratively on a mixed-media recasting of Dante's *Vita Nuova*. Now he gives us *The Little Sailor: A Romantic Thriller*.

The Little Sailor (Daisy H Productions, 2005) is an attractively packaged, double-cd audio book,[201] which the author reads in a mellow, lilting baritone resonant with the timbre of New York's Italian

---

[20] In 2008 Bordighera Press published *The Little Sailor* in its first print edition. In 2011 Valerio published the title as a Kindle book.

colonies. Like most of Valerio's narrative fiction, *The Little Sailor* alchemically combines personal and popular cultural histories; but unlike the earlier work, this opus resolves the logic and emotion of its protagonist's episodic memory in a linear plot, transmuting the Little Sailor's childhood experience of his community (particularly its women) in the first section, "Brooklyn, Rome," into the action of second section, "The Bensonhurst Pigeon," a whimsical adaptation of Hammett's and Huston's *The Maltese Falcon*.

The Little Sailor exists only within the Italian American community from which his alter ego, Antonio da Brooklyn, finds himself estranged (as the "da"—Italian for from—suggests). In "Brooklyn, Rome" Valerio presents scenes of the Little Sailor's fascination with the community's women. This fascination begins with his mother, one of the many feminine deities to whose power he bears awed witness. For the Little Sailor, the "dark Italian widow" is the center of a muliebral universe. For Antonio, she is almost something else. "Naked, crawling from the foot of his bunk toward him the dark voluptuous woman was about to become an object of masturbatory fancy. But then, suddenly, she disappeared. After all, she was his mother." His mother, like Dante's Beatrice, is a fancy. While his Bensonhurst, like Dante's Florence, is both a myth and an incestuous, close, if not entirely closed, society. Beautiful, forceful women, from the prepubescent girl Thrill to the widow Mrs. Tanzi, whirl around him, becoming sovereign avatars. Because of them he will worship goddesses his entire fictional life. These women "opened him to the Sibyl's Voice of Truth, which told him of the mysteries, with room for his splendid, silent voice, but with no answers." They also allow him to carry his knowledge of "the mysteries" beyond Bensonhurst.

In several "goddess" vignettes at the end of "Brooklyn, Rome," and in "The Bensonhurst Pigeon," the adult Antonio encounters goddesses who, unlike the beatified Beatrice, are entirely human. The "Goddess of New York," a revenant of Lefty from *Lefty and the Button Men*, is all carnality, while Brigid O'Shaunessy, a goddess of cinema, is no longer the perfectly young and seductive Mary Astor. "Now she appeared as old as she was. Her figure was still svelte, angular, a bit more fleshy. The tedium of barbaric prison life had weighed on her back, pressing forward her shoulders, which, in turn, caved in upon her chest." The earthiest of Valerio's goddesses are the tough-talking, intrepid and imperious "Italianist Professor" Ellen Rothenberg, a. k. a. the Baronessa, wife of aged Antonio's Doppelgänger, the Fat Man; and the hunch-backed grocer's daughter, Frances Palermo, a character magically transported from the Little Sailor's Bensonhurst, around whom the tortuous plot turns. The double-voiced narrative reads like a wish for Antonio and the Fat Man to retain the Little Sailor's belief in goddesses' absolute grace and in the native community's mores, despite mounting evidence that both are, in the Buddhist sense, transient. On a trip to Sicily, the Sibyl tells Antonio, "'Suddenly, you felt like the five year-old boy but were really as old as Methuselah.'" For Valerio's men memory is life and life, memory; both are most powerfully experienced through women and their central role in communal ritual, and both are illusory.

Valerio's fiction has always scrutinized the interplay of life and memory in art, especially in film, from Valentino to the Godfather to Sam Spade, all of whom live somewhere between other characters' realities and their fantasies. In *Valentino and the Great Italians,* the autobiographical narrator claims, "Valentino had hundreds of children and I fancy I am one of them." In *Lefty and the Button Men,* Nicholas writes a story called "The Last Godfather," in which he kills off the Godfather figure and in the process transforms his confidant Johnny from movie gangster into wise Bensonhurst uncle. *The Little*

Sailor stars the characters of Valerio's youth alongside film idols of his and the Little Sailor's childhood. Since memory and cinema are equipotent simulacra, the Little Sailor's past becomes the future of the Fat Man, who half-realizes he will "achieve immortality, not through vast wealth, but through love for a woman," and who, on his way to solving the mystery of a jewel-encrusted bird,

> cast a glance out the right window toward the void where the Twin Towers had stood. Their wakes, their ghosts, seemed to still catch the new day sun's vermillion rays, glinting, reflecting about where the high windows and girders had stood, like a gorgeous woman's clandestine, reassuring wink at an admiring boy, saying: "Don't worry, kiddo. In the end, everything is going to pan out."

Here is the private, woman-filtered experience of communal life, Valerio's quintessential métier, the animating principal of his entire literary corpus.

The characters of this latest narrative, both those inspired by reality—Margherita, Mrs. Palermo, Carolyn Percascia, Mrs. Tanzi—and those lifted from film—Sam Spade, Brigid O'Shaunessy, Kaspar Gutman—in their grandeur recall the characters of the author's earlier books: his family members, Lefty, Johnny, Jack Cusimano, Pietro LaClacca, Anita Garibaldi, the Mona Lisa, Valentino. Valerio unites them all through refrains, such as text-to-text variations on "She was all of one great piece" or "A cluster of black hairs grew out of flesh-colored mole below her bottom lip, which she was always chewing"; and through running jokes like the one about New Jersey, which in *Lefty* goes, "Such a man was from everywhere in New Jersey," and in *The Little Sailor* goes, "New Jersey could have been everywhere." These characters play an ethnic *opera semi-seria,* whose major theme is cultural connection, disconnection, and reconnection; and whose logic, language and humor are those of fable: of a mythical Italian American homeland where a woman's lips grow thin from the lack of her husband's kiss, where pigeons refuse to fly for a boy's absence, where an immigrant matriarch marries her native city, and where the sun sets on the horizon of a beautiful hunchback's pregnant mound.

ONLY THE ZEN KNOW BROOKLYN
Diane di Prima's Parent/Poet Wisdom

These eyes of children
         windows
                  on our hope :
that
      ALL RESISTANCE IS
            TRIUMPHANT RESISTANCE.

All love
     is revolution

—from "Revolutionary Letter #69"

To conceive, to birth, to parent children beyond the pale of conventional society, to write of the struggle, to write against norms: These are profound acts of love and resistance. When our belly fires move us to raise children and write, we continue our line and help to purge a social system that has outlived its usefulness. For Diane di Prima, the Brooklyn Italian community of her childhood, as presented in the claustrophobic poem "Backyard" ("where no one opened the venetian blinds…and naked plaster women bent eternally white over birdbaths" (*Pieces* 114)) is one such system; Twentieth-century America is another. Listening to her grandfather, anarchist activist Domenico Mallozzi, the young di Prima heard the message, "We must learn HOW to love…if we do not, we will die: all the people of the world will die" (*Recollections* 13). In response, many of us learn love, love, and teach love, to redeem what we inherit.

Di Prima writes to redeem, seeing the life and work of the artist as blessed, as one long act of reflection, compassion, sacrifice, and renewal (103). In her Italian American community and in America generally, in her life as depicted in her work, she projects a spirit of community and compassion both Christian and Buddhist, giving birth to real and literary children who should not be fenced in as she was by her childhood Brooklyn house and yard, by the "peasant morals" (104) of her family. She redeems this peasant mentality by emphasizing the beauty of a magical order and by questing to understand this order, to find an American eight-fold noble path up a cobblestone village road, and in doing so to find "right livelihood" (Hanh 113 and ff.) in this society—escaping the "special kind of immigrant dysfunction" manifest in "the obsession with advancement, or in other words, The American Dream" (*Recollections* 110). For the artist, especially for the woman artist, this path must pass through parenthood, even if we assume that the artist's life requires a complete commitment to art; a fidelity to, in di Prima's words, "the unspoken perfectionism I took for granted—together with all my friends and fellow artists: the unspoken agreement to 'produce,' the tacit belief we held that our only value was in the Work itself" (262), which was the guiding principle of her life in New York City, that life itself a new Bohemian version of immigrant dysfunction. But how can a writer seek to redeem the world through the plan and inspiration that is art, and still parent the children who will execute the plan?

For this acolyte of Keats and "poet of reproduction" (Libby 47) the answer, as given in *Recollections of My Life as a Woman*—aside from having other parents watch her children while she visits lovers' apartments—lies in the Bay Area, where, on her first visit, during a party thrown by the assemblage sculptor George Herms, she "for the first time... knew it was possible to have it all. To have the children I wanted, as and when I wanted, and still to write poems. To live without struggle, or to have a different relationship to struggle" (*Recollections* 267). She records the rest of this epiphany in a style that eschews practical concern. "Watching these beautiful women with their babies, eating these figs, sitting among George's powerful work that seemed to grow of itself straight out of the ground, I then and there decided to have LeRoi's baby. To end my grieving at last, erase the abortion of last year, with the child of this. It was clear that it was my right. That I need ask no one's advice or permission, simply follow my Will, wherever it now led me....This insight was burned in my brain, my heart and gut, by the sun, the music. The overflowing love" (267). Although the young di Prima's plan might appear impractical, it grows from her self-conscious "romantic primitivism" (Libby 58) and adherence to the "solidarity of extreme individualists" (67) that is central to her artistic program. In a few sentences she successfully combines the Buddhist imperative to follow the four noble truths (Hanh 9-11) and eradicate the roots of present suffering, with the categorical imperative and a brand of European pastoral and Indo-European mysticism, which combination colors much of her later poetry, especially *Loba*.

Like other feminists of her generation, Prima champions concepts of family that defy convention (Kirschenbaum 54), in the face of scorn from any quarter, even from the era's unconventional New York literary society. She reports of her artist friends, that when she became pregnant, "Nearly everyone thought I was behaving badly" (*Recollections* 275). But she endures, finding productive ways to blend the roles of parent and poet by, for example, including her first daughter Jeanne in the first production (the fortuitously titled *Discon-*

tent) staged by the New York Poets Theatre. When she finally arrives on the West Coast, among San Francisco artists, the story is different. "In the San Francisco art scene," she writes, "there was a well-defined place for women and children, a way of taking the family into account, including them all in the picture of the bohemian life. This didn't exist in New York. I had myself blasted a niche of sorts into the stone wall, big enough to fit myself and Jeanne into the picture, and I knew it could be done, but it was hard. It took a certain stridency, a self-confidence that West Coast women might have felt uncomfortable with, or confused with arrogance" (*Recollections* 282). Here di Prima, a "fierce judge" as well as free spirit, not only calls her contemporaries to account, but also begins to consider her own balancing act. Aware that she could be strident in her personal life, she exhibits a concomitant vehemence in her work. She balances this vehemence, crystallized in *Revolutionary Letters*, with a command of language ("Ode to Elegance"), an encyclopedic reach ("Canticle of St. Joan"), and, on occasion, a sense of humor that universalizes her struggle ("No Problem Party Poem") (Libby 53).

Di Prima's vehement poems are legion. One fine paragon is this section of "Narrow Path Into the Back Country" (dedicated to the poet's close (then estranged) friend and fellow parent/poet Audre Lorde), the vehemence couched in artful phrasing, deft line breaks, and a buoyant voice.

> we endure. this we are certain of. no more
> we endure: famine, depression, earthquake,
>   pestilence, war, flood, police state,
>   inflation
> ersatz food. burning cities. you endure,
>   I endure. It is written
> on the faces of our children. Pliant persistent

> joy; Will like mountains, hope
> that batters yr heart & mine. (Hear them shout)
> And I will not bow out, cannot see
> your war as different. Turf stolen from
> yours & mine; clandestine magics
> we practice, all of us, for their protection.
> That they have fruit to eat & rice & fish
> till they grown strong.
> (Remember the octopus we did not cook
> Sicilian style/West African style—it fills
> your daughter's dream) I refuse
> to leave you to yr battles, me to mine. (*Pieces* 111-112)

On display here, in addition to di Prima's passion and skill, is her constant theme of the parent/poet as conduit of human continuity through creative power: her mandala.

Of course di Prima, like all new parent/poets, faces a period of adjustment. Visiting Mike Goldberg, he of O'Hara's "Why I Am Not a Painter" and of her own "Magick in Theory and Practice" (dedicated to Goldberg), she describes her experience of his apartment from a parent's perspective. "I was supremely uncomfortable there: it was all so beautiful and well arranged, and I was painfully aware that I had two totally wild and messy kids in tow. I did what I could to keep track of them (make sure they didn't write on the walls or spill stuff on the sofa), and at the same time write, house-hunt, figure out about money, and do what we now call 'damage control' with the entire New York arts community" (*Recollections* 349). The dropping in on artist at work that O'Hara is allowed becomes extremely difficult for Mama di Prima. She feels distant from the carefully arranged world of the painter. That distance frames her poem to Goldberg, which begins with the address, "to all you with gaunt cheeks who sit / glamourized by the sounds of art in the / last remaining lofts...," and ends with a complex image of farewell.

                                                   oh home
I may never see again   oh glamour
like Baudelaire fading in a long hall of mirrors
called past as I move backwards over
its back velvet floor. (*Pieces* 75)

The elegaic tone and grotesque image convey the poet's ambivalence: longing and freedom from another form of enclosure.

One might qualify di Prima's discontent in Goldberg's house by reciting the sequence of messy arrangements that seem to have formed her life—at least her life prior to full-time, permanent residence on the West Coast—but the new and permanent differences clearly extend beyond housekeeping and "damage" to reputation. In adjusting to these differences, di Prima echoes other writers who at first felt compromised by their decision to raise children (Emerson): "[The babies] became a ballast, an anchor. Some kind of necessary and opposing weight, and I stopped trying to fly so far so fast. In a sense, it was Jeanne and Mini who anchored me—kept me on the planet—and I knew it, even then" (*Recollections* 299). Grounded, cast as link in chain, she flies away from the sun and down to a studio abode. (Descriptions of her marriage and several living arrangements with Alan Marlowe in *Recollections* reveal great concern for the placement of desk in domicile (334, 354).) And in di Prima's state of stillness, the presence of children and the work "correspond," so that, she explains elsewhere, everything is "richer, constantly richer" ("Tapestry" 20).

While di Prima recognizes the practices of writing and raising children as equal fulcra of her life, she uses the Buddhist concept and practice of "right livelihood," of "earning your living without transgressing your ideals of love and compassion" (Hanh 113), to countervail the traditional European distinction between domestic women and women artists, articulated in her memoir by a Jungian psychiatrist named Maria Rolling, who tells her, "My dear...you are an intelligent woman, you write books. In Europe a woman such as you would probably not even *try* to have children" (*Recollections* 298). A practitioner of Yoga since the 1950s, di Prima has demonstrated time and again that she can manage nicely to parent, to write, to publish, and to maintain her independence from men. She has paid a price, of course, in uncertainty—continual drastic change and movement from one living arrangement to another, scant emotional and financial security—and in a toll on her family that a reader can only surmise. She claims that she lives through a constant "storm of regret" (346) over her choices, she and her long-time companion Sheppard Powell staring "at each other down long corridors of Art" (346). This price leads her to the conclusion that anyone who wants to lead a literary life should have "some kind of private income" (350), that the parent/poet can much more easily perform her high-wire dance with a wad of cash in each hand.

On the other hand, at a crucial time in her life as parent and poet, the combination of marriage, children, art and poverty have brought di Prima closer to her own parents, from whom she lived mostly estranged for years. This development in *Recollections* allows her both to send the kids off to live with them now and then, and to come to terms with the necessity of a "unifying principle in culture, art, history that was not only possible but *necessary*...on which I could hang my own experience, my knowledge," one like her anarchist grandfather's, which could "shape and inform my Will" (421). That unifying principle is the Buddhist way she has pursued since her youth. A reflection of that way, her later poetry hinges on the expression of wisdom hard won, the hallmark of her work from *Revolutionary Letters* forward. As should be by now apparent, I am particularly interested here in that wisdom as expressed in poems on the subject of the parent/poet.

In a recent essay, Tony Hoagland describes, by way of Wordsworth, what he sees as one of the two varieties of poetry, wherein poetry "is a means of gaining perspective on primary experience," in which "powerful emotions can be gathered, then dynamically relived, translated, and digested in the controlled laboratory of the poem—by proxy, such a poem also constructs perspective for the reader" (as opposed to poetry that seeks to disorient the reader and to challenge the very notion of perspective) (437). *Revolutionary Letters* and *Loba* are filled with perspectival poems, the perspective of the peacenik, free-lover, Buddhist, feminist, anti-capitalist, pre-industrialist, mythologist, Universalist, Italian. "Revolutionary Letter #4" presents a number of these perspectives at once.

> Left to themselves people
> grow their hair.
> Left to themselves they
> take off their shoes.
> Left to themselves they make love
> sleep easily
> share blankets, dope & children
> they are not lazy or afraid
> they plant seeds, they smile, they
> speak to one another. The word

> coming into its own : touch of love
> on the brain, the ear.
>
> We return with the sea, the tides
> we return as often as leaves, as numerous
> as grass, gentle, insistent, we remember
> the way,
> our babes toddle barefoot thru the cities of the universe. (11)

This poem depends for its effect on the existence of the unseen forces that do not actually leave alone the speaker's people, primal innocents described elsewhere in the collection as "Tribe" (*Revolutionary* 8). This is the tribe of anti-establishmentarians, the Learyites (of whom di Prima was briefly one), of those who believe in peace and the perpetuation of peace through the defiance of prevailing norms and through the act of procreation (literal and literary) in this spirit.

"Revolutionary Letter #22" begins with the question, "what do you want/your kids to learn, do you care/if they know factoring, chemical formulae, theory" (35). The absent question mark begs the question. The parent/poet must produce children who will redeem generations of human beings disinherited from the land and disconnected from their spirit selves, by giving them a simpler life of sex, belief and art unnamed as such; simply the daily acts of life which bring the rain, bring bread, heal, bring / the herds close enough to hunt, birth the children / simply the acts of song, the acts of power, now lost" (45). The wisdom of this life, being divine, is, as Wordsworth believed, the province of children. In "Revolutionary Letter #55" the speaker admits,

> All I can say
> is what my daughter age six once said to me :

> *'if I can't pronounce it
> maybe I shouldn't eat it.'* (71)

The example works fine here. In "Rant, From a Cool Place," di Prima plainly proclaims the philosophy inherent: "How long before we come to that blessed definable state / Known as buddhahood, primitive man, people in a landscape / together like trees, the second childhood of man" (*Revolutionary* 148). The child indeed becomes the father/mother of the man/woman, the poet's greatest inspiration and the principle of balance in the parent/poet's life. Children embody imagination. Thus, the wisdom of di Prima's most famous line: "THE ONLY WAR THAT MATTERS IS THE WAR AGAINST THE IMAGINATION" *(Revolutionary* 104).

Revolutionary Letters, her most cohesive and powerful collection prior to *Loba*, revels in the defiant stance of its speaker, by turns earnest and mocking. The poems of *Loba* are generally more circumspect and solemn in tone; still insistent on the ethos formulated in *Letters*, but more nuanced, narrative and spare. The speakers of these poems speak less *against* any establishment and more *about* legendary landscapes—di Prima was a student and anthologist of myths (*Various Fables from Various Places*)—inhabited by characters who enact lessons in the power of creation as the creation of power. The world of *Loba* resists placement in time instead of resisting the powers that rest in any one place and time. The wisdom is imparted through metaphor. The frame of reference is positive, one of "female subjectivity" (Giannini Quinn 185) in multivalent creation, tracing itself back to the Wolf Mother of Rome recast in new world language and at ease in a Buddhist sense of oneness with a transcendent feminine spirit and power. These poems represent di Prima's destination as parent/poet.

Loba embodies the parent/poet, so that most of this woman's epic is implied metaphor. "Loba in Childbed" presents the she-wolf fulfilling the timeless mission of renewal.

> She lay in bed, screaming, the boat
> carried her to the heart of the mandala
> sweat stuck
> hair to her forehead, she
> lay back, panting, remembering
> it was what she should do. (*Loba* 30)

In childbirth the mother is "carried" to the mandala, the reunification of self, which, in *Loba*, means reconnection with a universal spirit and purpose native to woman. The Loba births a totem, "round stone head monolith / lying in Columbian jungle," which "tried to articulate, to burst / out of her" (31). Di Prima equates articulation, the production of language, with birth, creation, so that the monolith is the seed of this creation, as described in "The Loba in Brooklyn": "Every man a seed syllable / every woman / its unfoldment (padma" (246). The padma is, of course, the lotus, whose male seed, usually submerged in muck, yields the female flower, "its unfoldment," a symbol of creativity and beauty, or art. Art regenerates, because it is one with literal procreation. Within the frame of a poem whose title recalls the origins of di Prima's struggle to reunify her self, the poet emerges from the cloak of Loba,

> To interpose my flesh between
>
> insensate rage &
>
> > the trembling,   well-ordered spheres. (248)

She will literally overcome "male rage" by using the male seed—here her grandfather's "voice I cannot remember… informing my life w/ such / impassioned speech" (249)—to bring forth the timeless, universal truth in language that can be passed down, because

> …sound is image
>   it occupies
> space
>   a shape
>   cast on the brain. (249)

So that the poet literally conceives the world, its children, and the language they will use to bring it back to an erstwhile organic state, whose loss she laments in *Revolutionary Letters*.

Di Prima has spun an entire ethos and aesthetic from the experiences of childbirth and parenting, combined with the study of history and the development of a hybrid traditional perspective. In so doing she has shown us a way in which parenthood can be not only a possible but also a revelatory part of the poet's life.

WORKS CITED

Di Prima, Diane. *Loba*. New York: Penguin Books, 1998.

———. *Pieces of a Song: Selected Poems*. San Francisco: City Lights, 1990.

———. *Recollections of My Life as a Woman: The New York Years*. New York: Penguin Books, 2001.

———. *Revolutionary Letters*. San Francisco: Last Gasp of San Francisco, 2007.

———. "The Tapestry of Possibility: Diane di Prima Speaks of Poetry, Rapture and Invoking Co-Responding Magic." Interview. *Whole Earth* Fall 1999: 20-22. Print.

———. *Various Fables from Various Places.* New York: G. P. Putnam's Sons, 1960.

Emerson, Sally. *New Life: An Anthology for Parenthood.* New York: Little, Brown, 2009.

Hahn, Thich Nhat. *The Heart of Buddha's Teaching: Transforming Suffering into Peace, Joy and Liberation.* New York: Broadway Books, 1998.

Hoagland, Tony. "Recognition, Vertigo and Passionate Worldliness." *Poetry* 96.5 (2010): 437-54. Print.

Kirschenbaum, Blossom. "Diane di Prima: Extending *La Famiglia*." *MELUS* 14.3-4 (1987): 53-67.

Libby, Anthony. "Diane di Prima: 'Nothing is Lost; It Shines in Our Eyes'." *Girls Who Wore Black: Women Writing the Beat Generation.* Ed. Ronna C. Johnson and Nancy M. Grace. New Brunswick: Rutgers UP, 2002.

Quinn, Rose Giannini. "'The Willingness to Speak': Diane di Prima and the Italian American Feminist Body Politics." *MELUS* 28.3 (2003): 175-193.

Ink in the Streets
Dana Gioia, the Four Types, and Italian American Poetry

Dana Gioia is a public critic writing, in his words, for "any intelligent person with the inclination to savor" the pleasures of poetry. In the past he has assessed contemporary poetry in terms that he hoped would satisfy the widest variety of readers and listeners, from New Formalists to fans of spoken word. In this new collection of essays he takes up the challenge again, offering compelling analyses and opinions that should spark ever more heated literary controversy.

Gioia's analyses of popular poetry and of (sometimes popular) Italian American poetry are limpid, insightful, and provocative. Reading William Jay Smith, he writes, "is like watching an elegant production of a baroque opera in which the world is suggested by a few spectacular pieces of Venetian stage machinery." Of California poets he asserts, "Although English is our language, it remains at some deep level slightly foreign to our environment—like an immigrant grandparent whose words and concepts don't entirely fit the New World." Throughout *Disappearing Ink: Poetry at the End of Print Culture* Gioia treats his subjects with the intricacy of thought and language they deserve.

In his 1992 book *Can Poetry Matter? Essays on Poetry and American Culture*, Gioia wondered not so much whether poetry could matter, but how—how it might "again become a part of American public culture." He recommended having poets read other poets' work; having arts administrators offer programs combining poetry with other arts; having poets write more prose about poetry; having anthology editors choose only work they really admire; having poetry instructors spend more time on performance than on analysis; and having poets and administrators use radio to expand poetry's audience. It was difficult to argue with these recommendations in 1992, and it still is. What was missing from them, however, was an acknowledgement of the performance poetry movements that had by then been thriving for years: spoken word since the era of the Beats, hip-hop since the 1970s, slam and new cowboy poetry since 1985 or earlier.

Billy Collins, the recent United States Poet Laureate and a gifted comic performer, adumbrates one of Gioia's central points about performance poetry in *The Spoken Word Revolution*, Mark Eleveld's and Mark Smith's multi-media spoken word anthology. "Another reason [for performance poetry's recent popularity]," Collins remarks, may lie in the oral reading's ability to return readers to a time preceding the dominance of print, when a new dimension of silence ... was added to the experience of verbal communication... the public reading is a throwback, a resurrection of the Romantic notions of spontaneity and genius as opposed to the modernist sense of the author as a reclusive inscriber of verbal patterns or, more extremely, the postmodernist sense of the author as a false construction.

Oral performance, the original impetus for poetry, has made it a celebrity and computer-age commodity.

Gioia sees culturally specific reasons for performance poetry's current popularity, and for its growing influence: the rise of new media and the resulting opportunities for local communities of poets to export their work. He points out that the shape of poetry is changing rapidly in response to a cultural shift from print media to audiovisual media: "recordings, radio, concert halls, nightclubs, auditoriums, bars, and festivals." The list should also include cable television and the Internet. In allowing and encouraging poets to reach large audiences without the benefit of print, these media have affected poetry's look and sound, and become part of its message. Within this new cultural context, Gioia goes about the business of categorization. Measuring poems by degree of reliance on performance technique or written text, he identifies "Four Types of Literary Poetries": performance poetry, oral poetry, audiovisual poetry, and visual poetry. Though not without merit, these categories tend to impose sensory boundaries that many poems do not respect. It would be difficult to pigeon-hole Billy Collins's "Nostalgia," Joy Harjo's "The Woman Hanging from the Thirteenth Floor Window," or Pedro Pietri's "Puerto Rican Obituary." Nevertheless, Gioia's categories do reflect the "factional politics" of the current literary scene; politics based on "assumptions about the artist's relationship to his or her own linguistic material."

Quite a few "popular" poets disdain the academy, and vice-versa, but Gioia's contention that "the term cowboy poetry still elicits snickers from literati, and most professors bristle at the mere notion that rap is a literary form" ignores considerable cooperation between the camps: For instance, in the 1985 anthology *New Cowboy Poetry*, Hal Cannon thanks the Fife Archive of Utah State University for continually making cowboy poetry "accessible to the public and to scholars." Gioia may also be overstating popular/academic polarization when he wonders "how much real dialogue about modern poetry now goes on between writers and scholars—even those teaching in the same university departments." The truth is that many poets these days, even spoken word poet/entrepreneurs like Bob Holman, if they are not full-time university professors, are visiting or adjunct professors who share opinions with their scholar colleagues. Still, Gioia makes a valid point: "Poets and theorists not only share no common sense of purpose, but they also increasingly lack a common language in which to discuss their differences." Although as many poets as theorists these days can speak the language of traditional prosody, few of either group are revising the aesthetic standards for evaluating the finest contemporary American poetry. The close readings that could update our critical vocabulary are not appearing, largely because poetry scholarship and explication (unless yoked to an ideological bandwagon) have become a professional dead end. Gioia's attention to popular poetry, then, fills a void in critical discourse.

Take, for example, his remarks on rap. When he observes that rap "characteristically uses the four-stress, accentual line that has been the most common meter for spoken popular poetry in English," and compares the Sugarhill Gang's early hit "Rapper's Delight" to Rudyard Kipling's "Harp Song of the Dane Women," he sets terms for appreciating hip-hop lyrics that a diversity of audiences can understand. Or take his remarks on the reemergence of narrative and formal poetry. He claims in "Disappearing Ink" and in "Longfellow in the Aftermath of Modernism" that contemporary popular poetry has reinvigorated narrative, meter, and rhyme. This significant essay not only reconsiders the poet's use of formal elements and of the long-abandoned long narrative poem, but also recasts a central theme of *Disappearing Ink*, the divide between "high" and "low" poetic cultures, in terms of Longfellow's profound popular influence and marginal critical reputation. Although most of us can quote a few lines of Longfellow, scholars and critics have excluded almost all of his work from the canon, just as they have neglected performance poetry. If anything, Longfellow's work has received even less recent academic attention. While a number of studies of rap and performance poetry have appeared over the last ten years, there has been only one scholarly book on Longfellow (Charles C. Calhoun's *Longfellow: A Rediscovered Life*). Like many readers, I encountered Longfellow in high school and college, and have not heard much of him since. Gioia's erudite reassessment of unfashionable poetry sent me hunting the shelves for both my old anthologies of American literature and my *Princeton Encyclopedia of Poetry and Poetics.*

In "West Coast Elegies," Gioia reassesses California's twentieth-century literary heritage. The cornerstone essay of this section, "Fallen Western Star: The Decline of San Francisco as a Literary Region," contends that San Francisco's lack of a publishing industry has damaged the city's ability to produce a memorable body of late twentieth-century literature. When it first appeared, this essay raised hackles, even eliciting a volume of responses *The "Fallen Western Star" Wars* (2001). "Fallen Western Star" and its companion piece, "Jack Spicer and San Francisco's Lost Bohemia," are important, but not necessarily for their account of San Francisco's literary culture. Their real contribution lies in linking the vitality of literary culture to employment opportunities, housing, and the state of urban Bohemias. For lack of adequate employment and housing, many writers find themselves shut out of the cities that have traditionally sustained writers. San Francisco and other California cities are just the longest-standing and most extreme examples. Missing from Gioia's account is an estimate of the Internet's potential for bringing scattered local (and national) communities of writers together. Though he asks, "Is the delocalized and disembodied cyberspace of the Internet the American writer's only alternative to New York?" he confines his answer to a contrast of Eastern and Western artistic communities.

In "Two Views of Robert Frost," Gioia calls on poets to emulate Frost's role as a public moral voice, a call that animates Section III, "All I Have Is a Voice." The section's title essay ponders society's continuing need for the consolation of poetry, especially in the aftermath of tragedies like 9/11. "In the days following September 11, millions of Americans needed poems strong and deep enough to articulate their sorrow, fear, and determination"; "American poetry will not outgrow its public responsibilities until there are no more weddings, wars or funerals." To which, as a poet or lover of poetry, one can only respond, Amen.

"What Is Italian American Poetry?" sustains a note that Gioia first strikes in "Disappearing Ink": the call for informed literary critics to write candidly and intelligibly about poetry. He rightly deplores that "most reviewers avoid negative or skeptical assessments" and that "much academic commentary on contemporary poetry is written in the professional language of academe rather than a public idiom." Like other bodies of creative work, Italian American poetry (and Italian American literature generally) have suffered from a lack of discerning criticism. A generation ago, when Italian American literature was still, as Robert Viscusi put it, "a literature considering itself," a body of work scholars were still recovering and discovering, this lack was excusable. The wheat had to be gathered, to be threshed. By the 1990s, however, scholars had harvested an abundant crop of Italian American writing, including the work of Italian American poets from Emanuel Carnevali to Rose Romano. Unfortunately, critics have written far less about Italian American poetry than they have about other genres. Over the past two decades, we have seen fiction, non-fiction, and mixed-genre anthologies, as well as a special issue of *Voices in Italian Americana* dedicated to drama, and *Italian Americana*'s symposia on fiction and film. We have also seen a number of critical studies, particularly of fiction and non-fiction narrative, but not a single anthology of Italian American poetry, much less a full-length critical study. Neither type of book has appeared, in fact, since 1994.[21]

---

[21] Since this essay first appeared, two such anthologies have been published: Dennis Barone's *New Hungers for Old: One Hundred Years of Italian American Poetry* (Star Cloud Press, 2011) and James Tracy and Tommy Avicoli Mecca's *Avanti Popolo: Italian American Writers Sail Beyond Columbus* (Manic D Press, 2008).

Neither has there been, as Gioia claims, much in the way of actual criticism. "No serious critic," he writes, "has yet surveyed the field with the necessary combination of knowledge, sympathy, and discrimination." Absolutely true. Encomium-laden articles and effusive reviews fill the pages of this and other Italian American cultural journals. Some of these pieces praise entirely deserving work; some of them praise or at least recommend mediocre work, as if it were bad faith not to root for the home team. Gioia declares that writing incisive criticism of Italian American poetry simply requires "resolve." It also requires adequate knowledge of Italian American literature, aesthetics, and culture. The literary corpus has now grown big and strong enough that some of the critics who have helped assemble it—Carol Bonomo Albright, Helen Barolini, Mary Jo Bona, Fred Gardaphe, Edvige Giunta, John Paul Russo, Anthony Tamburri, Viscusi, and Dennis Barone—along with a host of newer ones, can begin its dissection. Gioia's advice to these critics and to organizations such as the Modern Language Association's Italian American Literature Discussion Group, the Italian American Studies Association, and the Italian American Writers Association, is clear and good. Concentrate your efforts, because "critical esteem and sustained attention are earned one writer at a time."

Gioia's studies in Italian American poetry suggest he may lead the dissection himself. In that case he will need at least to reconsider his definitions of Italian American poet and Italian American poetry. He classifies it as a "transitional" body of work, and defines the poets as "first and second generation writers raised in the immigrant subculture." These characterizations fail to figure ethnicity as it is: a mutable cultural construct, especially as it manifests itself in poetry. They equate to an insistence that only poets who are African American and who were raised in the Jim Crow South or in the nation's ghettoes may be called African American poets. The real issue, as it was for, say, the very white-appearing and passable Jean Toomer, is voluntary identification and skillful recreation of one's heritage. Most published Italian American poets have to this point in history come out of immigrant subcultures. But some, like me, a product of the Long Island suburbs, and Donna Masini, a product of the Staten Island suburbs, have not. Then we may also need a redefinition of "immigrant subculture."

A recurrent theme of Italian American poetry is the dialectic between the impulse to preserve culture and the impulse to escape it. Gioia calls this dialectic a contest "between tradition and revolution," which I judge more a conflict between tradition and individualism, the desire to feel oneself, as Luigi Barzini phrased it, "a unique specimen of humanity," a desire which has always pervaded Italian culture. Either way, this tension defines the best Italian American poetry, including the work of Romano, Masini, Peter Covino, Gregory Corso, Diane di Prima, Sandra Mortola Gilbert, Maria Gillan, W. S. Di Piero, Rachel Guido DeVries, and Felix Stefanile.

Admitting he is no scholar of the field, Gioia limits his discussion to a few important Italian American poets, including Carnevali and Ciardi, both of whom deserve the critical attention he pays them, each of whom succeeds in creating a "private verbal universe" of culture. As Gioia sees it, most other Italian American poetry has been more concerned with the documentation of external experience than with the internal experience of culture as figured in private language. Since much mediocre Italian American poetry appears in print, I can understand why he might think so. But the fact is that a number of other Italian American poets have produced poems that far surpass documentary. To name just a few: the roll of poets I have just called, Kim Addonizio, Pascal D'Angelo, Barolini, Joseph Bathanti, Gioia himself, Elaine Terranova, Ned Balbo, and Michael Palma. An exploration of their private poetic universes requires much greater space than I have here, but it is a project we must undertake.

I hope that as one of our premier poets and critics, and as Chairman of the National Endowment for the Arts (he served as chair from 2003 to 2009), Gioia will continue to engage the work of other Italian American poets, which, at its best, is as intellectually, linguistically, and culturally complex as Italian America itself.

Maria Terrone's *Eye to Eye*

The eye is presence and memory, artist and collector of art, body and body part, defined by perception, always seeking resolution in reflections of itself and its vessel. Maria Terrone's third full-length collection begins with the painted eye on its cover, an "eye miniature" or "lover's eye," one of only a thousand or so that survive from a period lasting roughly from the 1780s to the 1830s. In 1785 the Prince of Wales, later King George IV, of England, commissioned a locket adorned with a painting of his own ocular orb. He sent it to a woman he was forbidden to marry, who, to avoid the situation, had fled across the English Channel. Soon, however, presumably under the locket's sway, she returned and became his wife. The practice became fashionable, as the far-flung enamored realized that they could now, with impunity, enjoy the intimate gazes of their distant lovers.

Eye to Eye (Bordighera Press, 2014) greets us with one such "lover's eye," one which can be found on the Salon.com Website, illustrating a 2012 article, "The Secret History of 'Lovers' Eyes'." This image and its presence on the Internet speak to the conundrums of perception and to *Eye to Eye*'s central concerns: the dialectical tensions between intimacy and distance, immediacy and memory, consciousness and freedom, the human body and the means of its transcendence. Across the book's four sections, other themes emerge in service of this dialectic: art's imperative to create an alternative reality, social media's imperative to distract us, and nature's promise to free us from the burden of perception.

The title poem is the first of many here that aim "to hold the private gaze / beyond the fleeting moment." The speakers of the first section, "Visitations," read what's lost to the present into present emblems of the past. In "To Begin Again," the speaker's fancy transports us to another scene, locating the liminal space of contemplation. "Open the New Year to 365 town squares," she implores, "and close your eyes / to picture the daily *passegiata*. / how surreal it would be to strut across / the cobblestones alone." This sort of space accommodates Terrone's considerations of time and its passage.

In this manner her poem "Swan's Wake" leads Yeats to Proust.

The swans have left

Their single-file parade has rounded
   the lake's corner,

out of view. They avoided
   my gaze as if they bore

beauty's burden, the guilt
   of *brute blood*

and *indifferent beak*
   that let Leda fall.

Such throaty talk among themselves,
   receding.

Here Yeats's unwearied swans are absent creatures of the word, in whose wake remain "a thousand yellow eyes, unblinking." The speaker is fully conscious that she dwells in the season after passion and conquest, a time when observation and consciousness reign, manifest in images and discreet ideas set off through deft enjambment.

But this moment comes early in the collection, and gives way to poems in which birds of other feathers promise speakers freedom from consciousness. In the second section, "The Body's Way," the speaker of "Words to Unpin Yourself From the Wall" seeks escape from her Prufrockian self in "the wild commotion of small birds hidden," wishing "To be inside one feathered throat pulsing and the vortex / of autumn leaves pulling the last light to itself." This will to avian life elevates Dostoevsky's "insect life," that is, the life given to action, free from the consciousness of being and of right and wrong, of time and memory, and of mortality. It is a desire distilled in the sharply associative "Country of No Gridlock."

> Duet of birds hidden
> beyond the white, fern-imprinted sky.
> 	I am grasping
> even in this vastness.
> Even as I try to leave
> my mind's clogged byways behind.
> 	I am grasping
> To learn how to unclench:
> this is what I must do.
> To be a small green thing,
> unfurling.

These birds, like many of the others in this collection, are hidden—in trees, in dreams, in vastness—elusive, but always an aspiration. This aspiration of "Envying the Birds" (the title of the most direct of the bird poems) is the desire for sensuality that submerges the perception of sensuality, an aspiration doomed to disappointment. This disappointment moves Terrone to explore other means of transcending the limitations of human mind and body: art and social media.

The third section, "In Disguise," takes art and artifice as its subject, while displaying the poet's mastery. In this sequence Terrone's concern with art and her technical acumen recall Dana Gioia and John Hollander; her unflinching observation of human frailty and the wages of transcending it bring to mind Tracy K. Smith and Claudia Emerson. "Becoming Silver," a trio of well-wrought sestets, gives us human beings making themselves into works of art. These living statues "remain unmoved, / Pygmalions who've tried / to make their own flesh stone / eternal as the carved guardians of tombs." This project of transcending the mortal coil, trying to create a "place apart" from the rest of humanity, still ends in the company of death. In "The Gargoyles Rebel," works of art decide to leave their "lofty cathedral perches," to trade their existence as *a conduit for medieval ideas* for something akin to fleeting but precious human life, "pressured to bursting, cracking, / teetering on the edge." But the tension between humanity's life force and art's transcendence of human frailty goes largely unresolved.

Any resolution of that tension derives from Terrone's own art, especially her gift for sound, in lines spare and expansive. The opening lines of "Becoming Silver," only eight to ten syllables each, pop with rackety consonance that echo its subject: "Faces forged to a new coin's hard dazzle, / they stand rigid on hidden stilts / above the piazza, unblinking." Terrone's lengthier lines are just as sonorous, like these from "Models & Marie Anoinette: Two Escapes."

> I take in a stripped-bare space, commercial buzz, the motion
> of flouncing baby dolls, lace bra the black center
> of a blinding white circle, and cheekie, I assume,
> behind the tripod. The image flickers across my retina

So we are back to the eye, to images married to music these images might make.

Many of the poems in "Crossing the Gulf," the book's closing section, deal with spatial, cultural, political and personal distances. This focus heightens the urgency of transcending confinement to our bodies. In the ingeniously conceived poem "Knives," Palestinians and Jews "whirling in chaotic space" overcome the dictates of their ethnic identities by using their knives only to cook. In "Across the Gulf," the speaker uses her eyebrows to try and bring her aged father back to the world. In "Lace" and "The Tattered Handkerchief," Terrone finds in generations-old Mediterranean linen and lace, "a map / to trace your way home," a path to the lives of her Italian forbears. But the most poignant attempt to reach a person who cannot be touched comes in "A Facebook Page in Iran." On line the speaker encounters someone named "Mohsen, trapped / there and he knows it" (in lines that avoid the technical cliché of internal rhyme by employing near rhyme). She cannot read the majority of his Farsi posts, but when in English he mourns the death of Whitney Houston, she "wanted to say: oh yahoo dot com friend, / oh Rumi-quoting poet, oh beardless infidel, / post and post again to burn the tyrant's Rulebook." The poignancy here lies in the want, in the consciousness of constraint, and in the artificial eye, which, like Prince George's, peers across gulfs of time and space.

Maria Terrone's *American Gothic, Take 2*

The evil of banality lurks "like ax murderers" in a recycled cardboard takeout cup, in "Muzak stuck on hiss," on a spouse's computer as "his eyes read the monitor / like a love letter," inside a grocery clerk screaming "'VOID!'," and in a series of phone messages "lying in wait / on your bedside phone." Maria Terrone wrestles this insidious spirit into the light, in her chapbook *American Gothic, Take 2* (Finishing Line Press, 2010).

One of the slim volume's stronger poems, "Erasures," shows us those sinister phone messages reducing human voices to "mere scrawls on bottled scraps," which do not merely wake or drown us, but "chop life to pieces." In an American life long on contact but short on connection, words mangle and are "mangled," an adjective that the speaker/poet of the opening ars poetica "Scraps" applies to one of her discarded drafts recycled in a takeout cup. The cup that has claimed the speaker's words is itself a mundane objet d'art, "an Acropolis cup of Aegean blue," about which this now short-order artist concludes, "I offer America my own moveable feast." As other personae do here, she manages to redeem violent or violated language through the whimsical humor that also animates Terrone's earlier collections—*The Bodies We Were Loaned* (The Word Works, 2002) and *A Secret Room in Fall* (The Ashland Poetry Press, 2006). Whereas the humor of those earlier books blunts the force of concussive loss, here it soothes the inflammation of inconsequence.

In the manner of Mark Strand, Terrone extends metaphors to explore the labyrinths of existential angst. She does this to best effect in the rangy "The Beatles Throw a Party in an Ancient Temple." This prosy poem's controlling metaphor is a dream, of a party thrown in an "ancient Eastern temple open at both / sides, where steps descend into reflecting pools." Most of its lengthy lines describe the Fab Four's unconscious "soiree," as a means of transcending a fearsome epiphany.

> When I walk down the street or descend into the
> subway, I am not thinking of antiquities and the
> tragedy of their destruction but how I can be saved
> from destruction—by terrorists, or time itself. *It is not
> dying.* I am no longer young.

The scene leaves the speaker and us with an image of impersonal comfort,

> …surrounded by the idols of my youth, all of
> them youths, too, all still alive, bobbing their
> heads up and down as they hobnobbed with their
> guests. *It is not dying.*

So any attempt to escape our fragility is as much an italicized wish as the neat unpacking of a dream.

Although Terrone has in the past exhibited a formalist touch as deft as Elizabeth Bishop's and a knack for the arresting turn as keen as Margaret Atwood's, in many of these two dozen poems she prefers unassuming structures ("A Star Looks Down on the Oscars") and straighter lines of thought ("At Land's Edge"), which balance a variety of generally deliberate figures. A stanza from "Means of Travel" typifies the volume's modest approach to form and theme.

Spectacles of Themselves—153

> Now I'm back, wingless, finless,
> wondering how to live.
> Better to stumble to the edge
> of each day and teeter there,
> camping far back in camouflage?

The question implies an imperative that concerns us all and that finds an artist in Terrone entirely conscious of its importance: how to will into being "a string that you follow" through the everyday.

Tullio Pironti's *Books and Rough Business*

A left uppercut from eighteen year-old Tullio Pironti, and down goes Tongo Troianovich. Pironti has KO'd a man with a reputation. At this moment the young pugilist loses "any sense of being the downtowner outside the stony blocks he knows best." "Now," he writes, "I belonged here, so fully that I became ringmaster. I finished the fight by giving the other guy a lesson: his own bruising Guide" [sic]. Later in *Books and Rough Business* (Red Hen Press, 2009, translation by John Domini; published in Italian as *Libri e cazzotti* [Pironti Editore, 2005]), Pironti, now an established publisher and bookseller, again becomes ringmaster, this time giving a different sort of sparring partner, the northern journalist and critic Grazia Cerchi, a lesson in the virtues of Napoli. She has come reluctantly, fearfully, disdainfully to the southern capital, to profile Pironti for a Milan-based magazine. "If you're going to write about Pironti," he tells her, "you need to know about Naples." Playing Virgil, he then guides her tour of the Inferno, of, really, his polis's treasures, a task that reflects his life's work: publishing "history in the streets," battling the corruption and organized crime that "remains a blight" on his country, and "carving out a place for Naples in the arts."

After running his own bookstore, Pironti takes over his father's shop in Piazza Dante (to which he still makes the brief commute by funicular from the hilltop Vomero quarter). His courage, native talent for improvisation and sense of *spettacolo* lead him to publish *Munich '72: Night of the Fedayeen* (1973), a book about that year's Olympics tragedy. Around the same time Libreria Tullio Pironti publishes *Metaphorein*, a short-lived but influential philosophy and sociology review. Pironti then builds Pironti Editore on the pillars of investigative journalism and literature—publishing, for example, *Il Camorrista*, by reporter Giuseppe Marazzo (1983) (the film (1986), from a young Giuseppe Tornatore) and the Italian translation of Naguib Mahfouz's *Cairo Trilogy* (1989, 1990, 1991). When he publishes *The True History of Italy*, a documentary account of the nation's Tangentopoli ("Kickback City") corruption scandal, he confronts a giant of Italian politics. Officially out of office when he summons Pironti to a meeting, Giulio Andreotti, a former career-maker or destroyer (and subject of the 2008 film *Il Divo*), remains formidable. With characteristic economy, precision and courage—traits of a good writer as well as a good boxer—the author fixes the power broker in a single image: "his lizard-like mouth, his lips serrated and dry." For his courage in publishing exposés, Pironti pays a high price: continual fear of assassination and actual house arrest, ordeals that earn him colleagues' esteem and yield "heartening proof that I'd done some good around this city and beyond."

If Pironti's tone is sometimes self-congratulatory, his work with Andy Warhol and other artists, to relieve 1980 earthquake victims, and other contributions to Naples's cultural renaissance, have won him that right and the affection of his *paesani*. The author returns this affection in attention to the city's local vocabulary (*"scugnizzo"*/"street urchin," *"guainella"*/"street fight," *"cu' 'o sfizio"*/loosely and in a certain context, "with a notion," *"guappo"*/"wise guy," *"ejj avant"*/"out of the way") and in streetwise historical memory. As a young man Pironti rides through one of the city's erstwhile exurban bowers and a current Camorra stronghold, Secondigliano. Post-War Italian legislation has encouraged urban sprawl that is burying the greenery of Secondigliano under ugly blocks of boom-funded and

Camorra-filtered projects. Pironti notes that to a Neapolitan the name "Secondigliano" holds "a touch of defiance," in calling to mind not only the failure of government, but also a "second hole, an early case of intravenous injection, punched in the buttocks of an eighteenth century king." This is history in the streets.

A witness to the Fifth Army's liberation of Naples—whose aftermath Curzio Malaparte's searing 1949 novel *The Skin* (republished in 2013 by New York Review Books) so brilliantly portrays—as well as publisher of American writers like Raymond Carver, Bret Easton Ellis and Don DeLillo, Pironti recently remarked, "I have always had a weakness for American literature, from when I was a boy. I was shaped by authors like Jack London and John Steinbeck…not to mention the unsurpassable and unsurpassed Hemingway." In fact, Pironti has published not only American literature, but also commentary on it, such as *Dopo Hemingway (After Hemingway)* (2000), by his friend and colleague Fernanda Pivano. And his interest in America extends to American readers of his memoir, a text that often uses Hollywood movies as points of entry into Italian history and culture.

John Domini's translation brings Pironti's story to America. The challenges of so doing begin with the book's Italian title. *"Cazzotti"* means either "rough business," "blows," "punches" or "fists." To my mind the last two options work best as images of the determination and danger underlying Pironti's career. Domini prefers the first option, abstract but true to the subject: the world of publishing in a city and country wavering between parochial feudalism and global capitalism. I defer to Domini, not only because he is a valued colleague, but also because he has made a life-long study of Neapolitan culture, whose fruit includes two recent novels, *Earthquake I. D.* (Red Hen Press, 2007 (published in 2009 by Pironti Editore as *Terremoto Napoletano*)) and *A Tomb on the Periphery* (Gival Press, 2008). Domini renders Pironti's prose in organic English, leaving traces of Italian for effect; and embellishes sentences for the sake of, in his words, "cultural illumination." Maria 'a longa, a cigarette vendor from post-War Piazza Dante, is, in Pironti's words *"la venditrice più popolare di Napoli,"* "the most popular saleswoman in Naples," because she vends single cigarettes from her cleavage, and in so doing takes a lead followed by *"altre donne senza vergogna,"* "other shameless women." In Domini's translation, these women are less *"audaci,"* "audacious" than enterprising: "[B]efore long a number of other full-bodied Neopolitan women were using the same trick. Thanks to our Maria…it no longer carried the burden of shame." This rendition allows that at a time when "coins were all they had to get them through the day," these *donne* simply acted as good, resourceful Neapolitans.

Like Jordan Lancaster's excellent *In the Shadow of Vesuvius* (Tauris Parke, 2005, 2009), *Books and Rough Business* reminds us that from its birth as a Greek colony through the nineteenth century Naples was one of Europe's cultural capitals. But Pironti's memoir goes beyond cultural history and guidebook. It offers an insider's perspective on the South's struggles and on Italy's continuing quest for functionality as a nation of people whose first allegiance is to their *paese*, not to their nation. It tells the story of a man's, his city's, and his country's coming of age by ascending through the realm of contemporary media and market-driven culture, all the while clinging to their souls.

Michael LaSorsa Steffen's *Heart Murmur* and Marcus Rome's *And This is What Happens Next*

Shelley understood mutability, accepted the oblivion that even the most gifted of us face. Keats could never quite give in. The best poets since his death—a line that runs in English through Yeats, James Wright and Philip Levine—have followed Keats in his quest for some transcendent truth of human existence in beauty, in art. Their best work charts life's "Hard Passage," the ultimate human reality and a section title of Michael LaSorsa Steffen's second collection of poems, *Heart Murmur* (Bordighera Press, 2009), winner of the 2009 Bordighera Poetry Prize.

The title of another section is "Vicissitudes," a string of unrelenting changes, mutability. Many of this poet's speakers describe their experiences of mutability and their attempts to find solace for it, in the study of common life and in the alchemy of language; even as they realize, like the speaker of "Creative Loafing," that their efforts will probably prove futile, that "My house if falling apart; a wooden fence surrounds it, / as if to contain my vicissitudes / grazing in their paddock." Other poems remind us that language is an attempt both to capture the world and to keep it at bay. The speaker of "Get a Life" sees in the title figure of speech "[t]he very idea that a life could be sanctioned or dismissed," before describing "the woman who still lives with / her mother and collects coins from France," who is not unlike the most transcendent artist, in that her fate is to "hit the bedrock of normalcy." The poem typifies what's best about *Heart Mur-*

mur: a human being's stubborn faith in the constant quest for beauty as resistance to loss.

LaSorsa Steffen skillfully employs a variety of forms to contain this theme as well as his visceral images and vigorous language. The forms in *Heart Murmur* range from long-lined, single-stanza poems in the manner of C. K. Williams ("Specialties of the House") to the tight tercets ("Vengeance") favored by the editors of *Poetry*, one of the top-flight journals in which the poet's work has appeared. Complementing his concern with form is the motif of mathematics. Several poems of the first two sections consider math ("Equations" and "String Theory") as an ineffective means of controlling entropy. "Like God" addresses the problem of this approach, its speaker confessing "Math to me, is / omnipresent, but not real. Like God." As in Ronald Johnson's *Ark*, the conundrum of human exploration remains that calculation and science at some point require faith.

Heart Murmur, in fact, offers a spiritual survey of the American landscape (as the other two section titles, "Indulgences" and "Like God," suggest). This survey radiates outward from Buffalo, LaSorsa Steffen's hometown, itself a rust belt Ozymandias. From that tough city spring the poet's working class, rock 'n' roll mystical personae poems, which balance his flights of calculation. The most memorable of these are "Cars" and "Metal"; the least, "Spacious Skies," a knock-off of Bruce Springsteen's "Empty Skies." In these and other poems, LaSorsa Steffen's everyman voice is frank and streetwise, now and then wistful and sweet, reminiscent of both Kim Addonizio and Gerry LaFemina. And like these two contemporaries, he can sing (in poems like "Still Point" and "Close Enough") poignant songs of the passage that even Keats couldn't resist.

The pronouncements and strategy of Marcus Rome's *And This is What Happens Next* fall far short of the soul and skill of *Heart Mur-*

mur. In many of these poems, Rome establishes promising scenarios, only to settle for simplistic turns, easy ironies or political pronouncements. "Professor" begins,

> Prof. Mario Piccolo
> the immaculately attired
> bespectacled museum curator
> prowls the dimly lit corridors
> in soft silent cotton slippers
> after hours
> alone and unseen.

The characteristically short lines paint a suggestive picture. The poet gives himself plenty to explore, but concludes with two stanzas that settle for caricature.

> He sits on the royal throne
> a golden sceptre in his hand.
> His head upturned and askance
> he dismissively waves his arm
> across the empty chamber.
>
> He tires
> and retires to his warm bed
> where he dreams his special dream
> of being a museum.

Leaving aside the poem's overuse of adverbs and either amateurish or ill-advised use of the word "special," even I, who have had often to find my way through a forest of professorial egos, was little surprised or delighted by the punchline: The professor is lonely and self-important.

Rome does offer us something of value in his use of refrain and anaphora. In his less strident poems— among the number ("A Trace of Doubt" and "Bon Appetit," for example) in which the speaker stands firmly on a soapbox—refrains of simple observation gain significance from shifting context. In "The Dealer to the Table" variations of the refrain "you came in here to give it up / not to take it home" allow us insight into the gambler's need for uncertainty.

Like most poets, when he is less conscious of the important philosophical utterance and more focused on concrete detail triggering emotion, Rome, a practicing psychoanalyst, is better. This is particularly the case in family poems such as "The Secret" and "Zen and Aunt Ida's Alphabet Soup." The infirm aunt of the latter poem "turns and turns back / to the flowing river / today like yesterday until tomorrow," modeling the sort of quiet way to truth that would improve most of the other poems here.

Fred Misurella's *Lies to Live By: Stories*

In one way or another, the stories in *Lies to Live By* (Bordighera Press, 2005) resemble the work of many writers, but of no single writer in many ways. Like James Baldwin's *Going to Meet the Man*, *Lies* documents intimate relationships within American communities undergoing the profound social changes of the Cold War era. Like Tim O'Brien's *The Things They Carried*, "Short Time," the centerpiece of *Lies*, which was previously published as a novella (Bordighera, 1996), presents the surreality and trauma of the Vietnam War. And like the fiction of John Fante and, more recently, of Anthony Giardina, these stories portray the inner turmoil of Italian American men and women living inside and outside of their family circles.

The circle is a universally familiar symbol. By definition it is either "a closed plane consisting of all points at a given distance from…a center" or "the area within which something acts, exerts influence" or still "an argument ostensibly proving a conclusion but actually assuming the conclusion as its…premise." When the circle is a symbol of family life, the terms of these definitions are themselves hard to define, as Fred Misurella's well-crafted plots and careful renditions of consciousness reveal.

Misurella's narrators and characters recognize that the centers of their lives lie inside their family circles, though they can never quite pinpoint these centers. Silences, secrets and strictures—the invisible forces that hold the circles together—frustrate their attempts to reconcile desire with family expectation. Joey, the melancholy narrator of "Body Lessons," describes in painful detail how life with his parents has kept him from coming to terms with his own obesity, with physicality in general, and, ultimately, with death. As a child he tries to confront bodily frailty in the forms of a disemboweled chicken and a corpulent cousin. His parents deflect his questions. "'You'll learn later,'" his mother insists, "'when you grow up.'" And we see that while she does indeed carry with her the knowledge of terrible loss, family custom permits her only to share bromides such as "'Beauty overcomes death.'" This strategy of protection backfires, however, leaving Joey still at war his own appetites, and able to identify death only as "something unknown and watchful advancing toward us," which he futilely prepares to fight off "with all my strength."

In "Body Lessons" and most of the other stories here, repressed emotions roil below a surface of steady voices and orderly narrative structures. Nick, the narrator of the collection's closing trilogy, its strongest stories, is forced to negotiate the treacherous path between his own powerful emotions, appetites and ambitions, and the equally powerful influence of family. Nick's family is Italian American, and as the narrator of another story, "Relations," complains, no one should assume that "being Italian-American…somehow lacks significance, or familiarity."

Through their depiction of family conflict in Cold War-era New Jersey and Pennsylvania, several of the stories in the first section, "Money, Love, Art," set the stage for the second section, the trilogy—"Macho Maudit," "The Dragon Lady and the Soldier," and "Short Time"—a novelette collectively titled "America." These three stories follow Nick from childhood through academic and sexual education to service in Vietnam and the disintegration of both his nuclear families. From the first page of "Macho Maudit" (which may be literally rendered as "Man Confounded") Nick is restless, looking to escape his family's plans for him "to live with and support [my father] and my mother until they died." He admits, "I needed independence and experience, but when I said that to my father one day he looked at me as if I were thinking about dating goats." As the rustic simile suggests, Nick's family lives by Italian village codes reapplied in America, in the form of what Herbert Gans labels "peer group society" and what Richard Alba calls "the family-based social circle," whose highest law is, in Alba's words, "loyalty to kin." To his own chagrin, Nick has internalized these codes. Studying a photograph of himself as a community college student—Several of Misurella's narrators study old photos for solutions to emotional mysteries—an older Nick tells us, "I look comfortable but not with life or my particular actions in it." In "The Dragon Lady and the Soldier," he admits that upon cheating on his hometown girlfriend, "Something—Conscience, God, or, one time I thought, all my dead ancestors—stared down at me and constantly shouted *No!*" The unhappy solution to Nick's family dilemma comes in the form of the Vietnam War.

In *A Terrible Love of War*, James Hillman explains that the attachments a soldier forms in battle tend to replace "All the former attachments in the roles of husband, father, son, even sweetheart," which for him "no longer have palpable power," because "[i]nside the utter chaos there is a structure of meaning, of meaningfulness, not to be found anywhere else." Nick confesses, "I had been happier in the Marines than I ever was at home, and I knew it." Misurella's command of military expression and his exemplary heart-of-darkness plotting convey the horrible impact of war on family life as well as the dubiousness of a soldier's self-knowledge. War doesn't make Nick any happier, but it does change his conception of family forever; just as his return from war literally and symbolically signals the dissolution of the circle he's always known. Back in the States, Nick's diminished family and community provide him only minimal comfort. Unlike the fellow Americans of Ron Kovic's *Born on the Fourth of July*, the living characters of "Short Time" are largely indifferent to the war and to Nick's experience of it. The dead, on the other hand, hold instructive secrets, which only he fully understands, and then only through narrative reflection. In the end Nick finds himself *almost* beyond his family's pale, but still there, believing, in the words of a key figure from his childhood, that "'you have to finish things right.'"

"Short Time" and the rest of Misurella's first-rate work here present a Freudian vision of individuals and families continually at war with themselves. For Nick and for many other characters, the price of fighting that war and surviving it, of stepping into the larger world, is the unexpurgated knowledge of mortality and the imperative to cope with that knowledge alone. In realizing this vision, Misurella displays many literary gifts. He handles both first-person confession ("Relations," "Body Lessons" and the trilogy) and third-person, single-character perspective ("Parenting," "Flames," and "A Man of His Time") gracefully; and, despite occasional lapses into explanation of their otherwise clear feelings, his narrators never wax maudlin about the tumultuous past. Misurella's dialogue is uniformly realistic and frequently wry, as in "Body Lessons," when Joey's mother tells him, "'You have to understand blood. And accept it. Now peel the potatoes.'" Pithy characterizations ("Mark was slight, short, stubborn. He showed an angry intelligence in his eyes that dared the world to test him.") and organic plots blend with the narratives' other fine elements to produce unassuming tales that offer foudroyant insights into Cold War American culture, into the difficulty of defining a family circle, and into the mind of the individual seeking to make sense of it all.

JOHN PAUL RUSSO'S *THE FUTURE WITHOUT A PAST: THE HUMANITIES IN A TECHNOLOGICAL SOCIETY*

Culture survives in language, in systems of symbolic communication stretching back as far as human memory. Culture in turn animates our lives. In this third millennium, computer technology is threatening to loose us from our cultural moorings, because its singularly ineffable code endangers the specific languages that anchor selfhood. Only by studying our specific languages and the humanistic wisdom they convey, by recognizing the enduring value of these vessels and their contents, can we maintain our humanity in an age of automated systems. This is the message of John Paul Russo's second book, *The Future Without a Past: The Humanities in a Technological Society* (University of Missouri Press, 2005): Broadly, "Western civilization is evolving on grounds other than its own, or on one highly specialized version of its own, the technological, and it will soon cease resembling itself."

In the first three of the book's seven chapters, Russo lays its philosophical foundation, building upon other critics' arguments, to demonstrate that if our attachment to literature and literary language continues to attenuate, over time we will lose our cultural memory, our ability to construct meaningful interior lives and to express our intricate thoughts to others. "Complex literary language penetrates the imagistic surfaces, probes into the furthest recesses of mind and feeling, breaks the force of habit, and draws patterns of coherence in order to deepen and empower a self-determining, continuously developing selfhood"; it "connects us to the past—personal, communal, and historical." Without it, we go "from being joiners to being viewers. Heavy readers tend to be joiners, whereas 'heavy viewers are more likely to be loners'." Seeking to universalize experience by favoring technique over content, we submerge "real difference, which is individuality," personal and societal. Thus technology can give us civilization, but not culture, because only the tools of complex language allow us to recalibrate the machines we construct, inside of which we more and more frequently live. This line of thought is a needful stilling hand to the intellectual embrace of universalized, technocentric education, in such other tomes as Thomas Friedman's *The World is Flat* (Farrar, Strauss and Giroux, 2005).

The first portion of Chapter II, "The Great Forgetting: Library, Media Center and Las Vegas," describes the consequences of deliberately forsaking our attachment to literary language, to the knowledge of history and its application to our present situations, to humanistic tradition. For Russo, the problem at hand is "the blurring of the line between high and popular culture." It is a problem that grows from our tendency toward visual transmission and multiculturalism. "Mediocre films based on novels often supplement the teaching of those novels, wasting valuable time....Memorization is out-of-date, and desperate for student enrollments, teachers reduce themselves to the lowest common denominator...." This point will resonate with anyone teaching at the college level who has complained, in not so many words, that today "Equality trumps quality: everything big or great— social elites, major artists—are lumped together and must be cut down to size, even though the artists earned their way by their own merit." Of course, the degree to which one accepts this assessment may reflect the degree to which one accepts the received canon.

The fascinating second portion of "The Great Forgetting" examines Las Vegas as a symbol of both the "presentism" described above, and "technicism": the technological collapsing of both time and space, the transformation of complex cultures into simple commodities produced for entertainment markets. As such a commodity, a culture loses its humanity, and we lose its value. This "whole process of desymbolization" robs us of our desire to engage a culture at its deepest levels. By allowing us to take the "Virtual Grand Tour," Las Vegas reduces the real thing, with all its potential for teaching us enduring lessons of human existence, to a mere "advertising marker for luxury, style, leisure, sexuality, and globalization itself." One need not be a Europhile to understand the loss.

In "The Circle of Knowledge," the third chapter, Russo details the history of the traditional humanistic curriculum, emphasizing its development from Cicero to Petrarch to Vico and Descartes, and its defense by Arnold and others in the face of ever-increasing institutional emphasis on training in the sciences and technologies. The last 150 years of this history is a story of technology's breakneck pace of development and the resultant great migrations of peoples and scientific ideas into our education system. A system about which Russo pessimistically concludes, "[W]hen we live entirely under technological conditions...a genuine humanistic education does not take root in students' lives at sufficient depth so that it can survive and sustain them through their careers." This pessimism may be a product of Russo's cultural conservatism, which elsewhere in the book places excessive faith in the traditional cultural constructs and core texts of Western society, and places little faith in humanity's ability to assimilate technology to its higher purposes. Or it may be entirely justified. He wonders, " Does [students'] inability to grasp, or indifference to, the so-called universal constants of human nature mean that those universals are no longer in force, but that a new very different humanity is coming of age?" In pondering these questions, we must also ask others: Is the periodic development of "a very different humanity" a terrifying prospect or just a regular feature of human history? How vociferously should protest the loss of cultural competencies? Are those competencies truly "constants" or are they variables?

The four chapters that follow explore these questions and others through examinations of literary genres, literary critical methods, and specific works of literature. The most powerful and original of these examinations is the final chapter, "Don DeLillo: Ethnicity, Religion, and the Critique of Technology." As a number of other critics have done, Russo begins at the flashpoint that is Gay Talese's 1993 essay, "Where Are the Italian-American Novelists?" He treats it, however, more carefully than anyone else has to date, quibbling with Talese's definition of Italian American literature, and making the case, as Fred Gardaphè, Linda Hutcheon and others have, for literary crypto-ethnicity. This discussion leads to an analysis of crypto-ethnic and blatantly ethnic themes in DeLillo's masterpiece, *Underworld* (Scribner, 1997), especially as they serve as antidotes to the novel's great preoccupation, technology. These themes include tradition, family, the "religion of the home," hard work, the child, mutual aid, realism, nostalgia, a sense of limit, fatalism, anarchic individualism, violence, sports, spectacle, leisure, memory, immanence, "Tame Death" (the easy acceptance of death as part of life), and belief in the afterlife. Although most of these themes are common to many cultures, Russo succeeds at showing how DeLillo, the product of a Bronx Little Italy childhood and extended Jesuit education, reaches back for sustenance to his roots and to the humanistic tradition of art as humanity's other great means of transcending the state of "death-in-life" to which technology often reduces us.

On display in all of these essays is Russo's broad and deep knowledge of humanistic philosophy and cultural criticism. "The

Tranquilized Poem: The Crisis of the New Criticism," for example, surveys the entire landscape of relevant literary theory, allowing the author, as he does throughout the volume, to punctuate critical summaries with his own trenchant observations. His view is always circumspect. Of the New Critics, he concludes, "For their ideal of synthesis, [they] looked backward. It was a vestige of the cultural ideal that traces through European romanticism to the seventeenth century, where it is already a nostalgic recollection of the Renaissance paradigm." Only a critic of Russo's learning can provide this invaluable perspective.

Of the dynamo Henry Adams wrote, "[I]ts value lay chiefly in its occult mechanism." Of technology Russo is saying the same. Like the dynamo of the nineteenth century, today's computer technology threatens to lure us completely from the mythologies from which we construct our selfhood and our society. He is arguing for a re-elevation of the humanities, of humanistic education, to harness technology before it harnesses the human race. And while he may on occasion sound too loud an alarm over technology's effect on our preservation of knowledge—I am thinking here of his take on university libraries and media centers—he does argue effectively that shifts in technology alter our encounters with knowledge, and that we can never substitute technology for critical thought. We must keep the humanities at the center of education and civilization, if we are successfully to cultivate our gardens, which, as Voltaire suggested, is the best way to manage systems that could easily dominate our lives.

ANTHONY GIARDINA'S *RECENT HISTORY: A NOVEL*

Like Luca Carcera, its narrator, Anthony Giardina's third novel, *Recent History* (Random House, 2001), asks a lot of difficult questions: Did the migration from city to suburb inaugurate the golden age or the decline of Italian America? What does it mean to turn personal experience into history? What does it mean to feel compelled to do so? In the absence of the male parent, can the child be the emotional father to the man? What is intimacy?

The first section of the novel, "Inca Boy," takes us through the 1960s childhood of tortured Luca Carcera. (The boy's last names derives from *"carcere,"* the Italian word for "prison.") One day, when Luca is eleven years old, his father, Lou, drives Luca to a spot "in the woods" outside Boston, where the "large, clamorous Italian family" into which Lou has married—He is also Italian, though not clamorous—is to make its new home. This family includes Lou's brother-in-law John, who soon establishes himself as the patriarch and principal social striver of the family, in spite of his rough edges. He sets the terms of the family "contract" to "make a neighborhood of Italians" among America's upper-middle class. But his plans help drive Lou from the family and lead to other minor tragedies in the course of Luca's youth.

Giardina's talent for interior monologue adds interest to a portrait of a suburban world painted more vividly by Cheever and DeLillo. Luca continually interrogates the ways of this world, which he believes have imprisoned his adult consciousness. At a barbecue thrown by his Uncle John, Luca reveals, "And here, it suddenly occurred to me, in this backyard, was life itself…But though I was close to it…it still seemed like a thing I didn't know how to get to, as though my allegiance, or else my deepest attention, had already been claimed by the other, watching side of myself" (75). He is compelled to question even the act of questioning, and to impose historicity and order on a youth reconstructed from disorderly memory.

Along with this compulsion, Luca suffers from acute sexual confusion and emotional paralysis, for which he holds his father responsible. "We are linked that way," he confesses, "two men who knew how to be absent from their own lives" (132). *Recent History* then is both a tale of two men's sexual and emotional educations, and a psychological study of those educations.

Giardina presents the second section of the novel, "History Teacher," as the outcome of Luca's youth. In this respect, the novel is a variation on the structure of Flaubert's *Madame Bovary*, noted by the narrator of Giardina's short story "I Live in Yonville" (from the lively, insightful collection *The Country of Marriage*). Because we have known him as a child, we may at least partially understand the adult Luca's romantic life and his reasons for living in fear of his past, which, of course, catches up with him. The resolution of the attendant crisis, not surprisingly, depends upon his father.

Although Luca, Lou and Giardina's other characters often speak as though they are awkwardly reading the lines of a forgettable play, *Recent History* does succeed in expressing the illusory nature of personal history, and furnishes a venue for Giardina's brave, sentient explorations of the minds of various Italian American men.

Dennis Barone's *Echoes* and *Separate Objects*

Philosophy and narrative are often, though not always happily, married. In Nietzsche, they become one; in Borges, they conspire in a fiction of unity; in Dennis Barone's *Echoes*, they vie for attention.

Like *Separate Objects* (Left Hand Books, 1998), a collection of poems, *Echoes* (Potes and Poets Press, 1997), a collection of "emblematic tales," concerns itself with connections and disconnections between writing and the philosophy of human existence. Through most of the pieces, Barone's narrators consider themselves as writers considering their thoughts and emotions as they echo from the objects and events of life. The narrator of "Biography," the collection's centerpiece, reflects, "You have realized the limitations of life: only so many languages, only so many places, only so many projects... Splintered by an unread text, the interpretation remains incomplete, unfinished. Objects, classification, order: repetition. Make an order out of disorder: repeat the process" (129). At its best, for instance in the pastiche apologue, "No Answer," this preoccupation with language and the literary process complements Barone's keen eye for detail and his good ear for phrasing. At its worst, it amounts to quaint postmodernism, to the narrator of "Biography" confessing to himself, "You have your heart set on obscurity," then following his heart.

In spite of its occasional pretensions, Barone's prose sometimes ascends to a level of poetry above the best lines of *Separate Objects*, approaching in tenor and quality the work of Charles Olson. "The Crossing," a meditation on waiting as a defining experience, and certainly the collection's strongest piece, displays the author's gift for the poetic expression of a mind (not) making sense of life's particulars. "The agony of waiting to see the one that you love: this is a theme that they should understand…Sing song, let's move along. Get going. Louisiana Hayride. Move along now. How much longer must I wait? It is 12:01. That man seated at the bar, that familiar looking man has gotten off his barstool, his high stool, his high horse, high school. He strolls; I sulk. Shit. How much longer must I wait" (69). Here repetition and rhyme lend Barone's prose the incantatory quality of thoughts in search of an end, love. Here words dance, albeit self-consciously.

The words of *Separate Objects* can also dance, but more than the prose of *Echoes*, closer in the footsteps of Olson and Eliot, they dance to the tune of death. "We thought / these bodies would /outlast / the years to come," remarks the speaker to the collection's most accomplished lyric, "A Poem for Daniel Davidson." "Now we see that / the passage of time is nothing to be / ecstatic about. / Print books / on acid free paper; shred / after sixty days. Please /work with what's here. / What does it matter that blue jeans were unknown to Cotton Mather? / 'spit it all away / slate / What does it mean that / all the poetry sounds like prose / or like a pose" (54-55). Barone sets the artist's worry for time lost to memorable music. His well-crafted staccato lines burst with intense speculation.

Language's inadequacy to express reality, thought, and emotion is the great theme of both volumes. Barone's prose and poetry both present a protagonist—the *rara avis* public Italian American intellectual—sounding the limits of effability. The speaker of "Proffer" enviously declares that "those who neither / professed nor practiced any religion / write without language." "Those" who pay little attention to philosophy and creed are better off than pitiable intellectuals, because they do not torture themselves with attempts at concrete expression in a mercurial medium. This is the issue that defines Barone's work and will likely define the reader's interest in it: Language may occupy us while we live, by allowing us to question life, but it may also divert us from living; and like the philosophy with which the author attempts to marry it, language rarely, if ever, provides answers.

Mary Bucci Bush's *Drowning*

At a *sui generis* conference on the writer John Fante, I had the good fortune both to hear Gay Talese speak about the dilemma of the Italian American writer and to read Mary Bucci Bush's *Drowning*. Talese claimed that women writers represented the promise of Italian American writing. *Drowning* (published as a chapbook by the Parentheses Writing Series in 1995 and as part of Bush's well-received 2011 novel *Sweet Hope* (Guernica Editions), a powerful story of Italian immigrants in the American South, proves Talese's claim.

Mary Bush's parable of Italian American-African American relations is set in August, 1905, on the bayou, an American purgatory of mud and water.

> Here, the water was wild. One day it was quiet and sweet and low; the next day it was pulling down houses and carrying mules away, or it was crashing from the sky in sudden, terrifying thunder and lightning storms, or it was seeping into everything through the ground that wasn't the solid ground it seemed to be.

More hell than heaven, this Dantean bog consumes its inhabitants—black and Italian immigrant sharecroppers. Water comes "from everywhere," puddles form as if by magic, and fish to inhabit them appear "from nowhere." Characters traverse the waterlogged land "itself turned into a patchwork of streams and ponds and puddles" where "even stepping on what looked like dry land became a risk." Unfortunately for these marginalized folk, even greater menaces lurk.

Drowning is told from the perspective of Isola, a young Italian girl who lives among statues of the Virgin Mary and black laborers singing amidst the cotton. Isola learns of a mysterious drowning from her black playmate Birdie, "probably the smartest person Isola knew." Isola's first imaginings of the victim leave his identity ambiguous; disfigured by death, he may be either black or Italian.

> [Isola] saw a big dark figure in her mind, the swollen shape of a man being pulled from the lake and then him lying on the ground, his wet clothes plastered to his bloated body while she moved closer and closer to get a look at his drowned face. But all she could see was a man sleeping, and she saw his puffy closed eyes and his puffy black cheeks and the diamonds of water glistening in his black hair.

Although later we learn more about the corpse's identity, Isola's indistinct vision hovers like an ominous shadow over the "bosc" (swamp woods) that Bush's characters inhabit.

Italian and black characters alike live in constant fear of their "American" landlords, who hold them in peonage and hunt them down if they flee. In this context the drowning of a dark man in the swamp's only benign body of water, a placid lake, suggests something more sinister than an accident. And when Isola and Birdie go together into the woods to learn the identity of the drowned man, what they learn instead is a lesson in the (sexual) brutality and divisiveness of American racism.

Ms. Bush spent months on the Mississippi Delta gathering raw material for *Drowning* and the novel of which it comprises one section. (Another section, "Planting," appears in Mary Jo Bona's anthology *The Voices We Carry*.) Her prose, likewise, gathers details of the bayou, the way one gathers wood for a fire: "The water was up in the woods, and the ponds were back. A few fallen limbs, cracked from the storm, their white insides shining, dangled from the trees or lay strewn in the weeds or low grass." *Drowning* is, in fact, a sort of Italian American campfire story, narrated from the wide-eyed perspective of a little girl, lent weight by its themes of bigotry and violence.

Bush's characters speak intelligible Italian American and African American language. Italian American characters speak a semi-literal translation of Italian, whose dignity recalls the dialogue of Pietro Di Donato's *Christ in Concrete*, while African American characters speak a Southern dialect that only occasionally forces the author to truncate beginnings and endings of words. By showing this sort of restraint, Bush keeps our attention focused on the story's themes and her own scrupulously elemental description.

The quiet realism of *Drowning* reflects both the Italian and African American traditions of silence in the face of oppression. Much of what happens is "a secret," a dark one, which promises to remain so. In telling this tale of secrets Ms. Bush seems to be asking whether or not Italians and blacks in America once found themselves in the same boat. When Isola tells Birdie of her parents' fear that "the Americans will shoot us," Birdie answers, "You dumb or something? White folks don't shoot white folks." It is this questionable distinction of Italians as "white folks" that finally drives Isola and Birdie, as it has driven so many Americans, apart.

INDEX OF NAMES

Acunto, Steve 92
Adams, Henry 171
Addonizio, Kim 145, 160
Alba, Richard 165
Albright, Carol Bonomo 144
Alighieri, Dante 106, 108, 120-121
Allen, Fred 14
Allen, Woody 80
Ambrosoli, Giorgio 72
Andreotti, Giulio 156
Antonello, Pierpaolo 73-74
Armstrong, Louis 4, 8-9, 11
Atwood, Margaret 153

Balbo, Ned 146
Baldwin, James 163
Barolini, Helen 144-145
Barone, Dennis 143-144, 174-176
Barzini, Luigi xiii, 44, 57, 64, 145
Bathanti, Joseph 145
Bell, Alexander Graham 60
Bell, Jeannie 36
Belmonte, Thomas 81
Bergman, Andrew 48
Berle, Milton 21
Berlusconi, Silvio 72
Bianchi, Stefano Maria 73
Big Bad Voodoo Daddy 25
Bishop, Elizabeth 153
Bologna, Joseph 77

Bona, Mary Jo 144, 178
Bonadella, Peter 67, 74
Bonaparte, Napoleon
Borsellino, Paolo
Bouchard, Norma 98-100
Bovasso, Julie 77
Boylan, Amy 73
Bracco, Lorraine 54, 70
Brando, Marlon 46-49
Broderick, Matthew 46-48
Brunetta, Gian Pietro 72
Bryant, Dorothy 115
Burnett, Carol 48
Bush, Mary Bucci 177-179
Butera, Sam 4, 11, 16-19, 21-24, 28

Calhoun, Charles C. 141
Calloway, Cab 14
Candido, Johnny "Candy" 8
Cannistraro, Phillip V. 117
Cannon, Hal 140
Carnevali, Emanuel 143, 145
Carter, Benny 8
Caruso, Enrico 76
Carver, Raymond 157
Casillo, Robert 30-31, 33, 36, 38, 67
Cassaro, Nancy 79
Cecchi, Emilio 87
Cerchi, Grazia 155
Chase, David 50, 54, 64, 69, 93
Chayevsky, Paddy 43

Spectacles of Themselves—181

Cheever, John 172
Chianese, Dominic 54
Cicero 169
Collins, Billy 139-140
Collins, Lee 6
Colombo, Joe 61
Coppola, Francis Ford 66-70, 94
Corcoran, Joseph 80
Corso, Gregory 145
Covino, Peter 145
Credence Clearwater Revival 24
Croce, Jim 24
Crystal, Billy 51, 68

D'Acierno, Pellegrino 14, 46
D'Angelo, Pascal 145
Dal Cerro, Bill 62
Dante, John 113
Davis, Sammy, Jr. 11
De Palma, Brian 67
Delbanco, Andrew 92
DeLillo, Don 92, 157, 170
DeLuise, Dom 49, 63
Demme, Jonathan 49, 81
DeNiro, Robert 31, 37, 39, 50, 53, 97,
Descartes, René 169
DeStefano, George 70-71
DeVries, Rachel Guido 144
Di Donato, Pietro 179
di Prima, Diane 125-136, 144
DiPiero, W. S. 145
Domini, John 155, 157-158
Douglas, Kirk 67
Durante, Jimmy 5

Eldridge, Roy 8
Eleveld, Mark 139

Eliot, T. S. 175
Ellis, Brett Easton 157
Emerson, Claudia 150
Eminem 25

Falcone, Giovanni 73
Fante, John 108, 163, 177
Ferrara, Abel 69
Ferrer, José 24
Flaubert, Gustave 173
Fratti, Mario 77
Frazzi, Andrea 71
Frazzi, Antonio 71
Friedman, Thomas 168
Fuller, Margaret 118

Gambino, Richard 55, 80, 95
Gans, Herbert 165
Gardaphé, Fred 30, 33, 69, 144
Garibaldi, Anita 115, 118-120, 123
Garibaldi, Giuseppe 115-118
Garrone, Matteo 71
Germi, Pietro 72
Giacosa, Giuseppe 89
Giamatti, A. Bartlett 113, 117, 120
Giardina, Anthony 163, 172-173
Gilbert, Sandra Mortola 145
Gillan, Maria 145
Gioia, Dana 92, 138-146
Giunta, Edvige 144
Goldberg, Mike 129-130
Goodman, Benny 9
Gotti, John 29, 92, 97
Gramsci, Antonio 71
Griffith, D. W. 67

Hack, Ed 107
Haley, Alex 93
Hammett, Dashiell 121
Harjo, Joy 140
Hawkins, Coleman 8
Hawkins, Yusuf 63
Hemingway, Ernest 157
Herms, George 127
Hijuelos, Oscar 108
Hillman, James 165
Hipkins, Danielle 72
Hoagland, Tony 132
Hofmann, Paul xiii
Houston, Whitney 151
Hughes, Howard 11
Hugo, Victor 115
Huston, John 121

Imperioli, Michael 54
Ingrasciotta, Frank 75
Innaurato, Albert 75, 77

Joffrey, Marisa 34
Johnson, Ronald 160
Jones, Spike 12

Kamp, David 3, 21
Keats, John 126, 159-160
Keitel, Harvey 31, 33
Kennedy, John F. 11
King George IV 147
Kipling, Rudyard 141
Kirby, Bruno 47-48
Kovic, Ron 166
Kuras, Lennard 34

Laake-Walsh, George 68, 70
LaFemina, Gerry 160

LaMotta, Jake 31, 43
Lancaster, Jordan 158
Landy, Marica 72
Lanzillotto, Annie 80
LaRocca, Nick 5
Lattuada, Alberto 72
Lawrence, Steve 48
Lee, Spike 36, 92
Lentricchia, Frank 92
LeRoy, Mervyn 67
Levi, Carlo 86
Levine, Philip 159
Liotta, Ray 39, 54, 70
Lombardo, Guy 8
London, Jack 157
Longfellow, Henry Wadsworth 141
Lupa 25

Madonna 25, 34, 83
Maggitti, Vincenzo 67
Mahfouz, Naghib 156
Malaparte, Curzio 157
Mallozzi, Domenico 125
Mangione, Jerre 5, 29, 99
Marazzo, Giuseppe 156
Marchand, Nancy 54
Marlowe, Alan 130
Martin, Dean 11, 84
Mascagni, Pietro 38
Masini, Donna 145
McCormack, Will 61
McCutcheon, Wallace 67
Mecca, Tommy Avicoli 143
Memmoli, George 31
Messenger, Chris 68
Meucci, Antonio 60, 117
Michalczyk, John 72

Migliaccio, Eduardo 76
Miller, Arthur 77
Milos, Sofia 57
Misurella, Fred 163, 165-166
Moe, Nelson 72
Moriarty, Cathy 37
Morosini, Emilio 118
Morreale, Ben 5, 29, 99

Nerazzini, Alberto 73
New Critics, The 171
Newell, Mike 69
Nicholson, Jack 49

O'Brien, Tim 163
Odets, Clifford 77
O'Hara, Frank 129
Olson, Charles 174-175
Orsitto, Fulvio 69-70

Pacie, Joan 83
Pacie, Ron 83
Palma, Michael 146
Palmentieri, Chazz 58
Paone, Nicola 12
Paparcone, Anna 73
Pastore, Vincent 54
Pavese, Cesare 57
Pellico, Silvio 106-107
Pesci, Joe 38, 39, 53, 70
Petrarch 169
Pickering-Iazzi, Robin 73
Pietri, Pedro 140
Pileggi, Nicholas 97
Pintauro, Joseph 77
Pironti, Tullio 155-158
Pivano, Fernanda 157
Placido, Michele 72

Powell, Sheppard 131
Prima, Leon 5
Prima, Louis 3-11, 13-28, 84
Proust, Marcel 112, 148
Proval, David 36, 54
Proyecto Uno 25
Puccini, Giacomo 89
Puzo, Mario 67, 94-95, 103

Rat Pack, The 11
Red Hot Chili Peppers, The 25
Red Shirts, The 118
Reitman, Ivan 58, 81
Renga, Dana 66, 68, 71-72, 74
Richardone, Bill 61
Riggio, Leonard 92
Risi, Marco 71
Ritt, Martin 67
Romano, Rose 143, 145
Romanus, Richard 37, 60
Rome, Marcus 159-162
Rosi, Francesco 73
Ross, Edward Alsworth 77
Roth, David Lee 24
Royal Crown Review, The 25
Rumi 151
Russo, John Paul
Russo, Richard 92, 144, 167-171
Ruvoli, Joanne 67

Santoro, Lara 69
Saviano, Roberto 73
Savoca, Nancy 81
Scaletta, Lenny 31
Scimeca, Pasquale 72
Scorsese, Catherine 36, 39

Scorsese, Martin 29-31, 33-37, 40-44, 52, 62, 69-70, 94, 97
Serling, Rod 43
Setzer, Brian 25
Shakespeare, William xiii, 29, 31, 44
Shanley, John Patrick 78, 81
Sharpton, Al 63
Shore, Dinah 21, 23-24
Sigler, Jamie-Lynn 55
Sinatra, Frank 3, 11, 111, 114
Sinclair, Ken 37
Smith, Keely 3, 10, 18, 21, 24, 27, 28
Smith, Mark 139
Smith, Tracy K. 150
Smith, William Jay 138
Socrates 102
Soldati, Mario 86-91
Sonny and Cher 24
Sordi, Alberto 72
Sorvino, Paul 40
Springsteen, Bruce 160
Stefanile, Felix 145
Steffen, Michael LaSorsa 159-160
Steinbeck, John 157
Stille, Alexander 73
Stockwell, Dean 49
Strand, Mark 152
Sugarhill Gang, The 141
Sullivan, Ed 11, 15, 17, 19-21

Talese, Gay 53, 170, 177
Tamburri, Anthony 68, 144
Taylor, Renee 77
Terranova, Elaine 146
Terrone, Maria 147-154

Testa, Carlo 73
Thomas, Danny 11
Till, Emmett 22
Toomer, Jean 145
Tornatore, Giuseppe 156
Tosches, Nick 3, 13, 18
Tracy, James 143
Turco, Marco 73
Turturro, Aida 55
Turturro, John 36

Valentino, Rudolph 111, 113, 115, 120, 122-123
Valerio, Anthony 63, 92, 94-96, 101-108, 111-123
Vecoli, Rudolph 93
Verga, Giovanni 38
Vetere, Richard 75
Vico, Giambattista 169
Victor Emanuel II 118
Vincent, Frank 38-39
Virgil 155
Viscusi, Robert 92, 94-101, 105, 108, 110, 143-144
Vittorini, Elio 87
Voltaire 171

Warhol, Andy 156
Welles, Orson xiii
Williams, C. K. 160
Williams, John 42
Williams, Tennesee 77
Witnesses, The 11, 15-16, 21-22, 24
Wordsworth, William 132-133
Wright, James 159

Yeats, William Butler 148, 159

Spectacles of Themselves—185

ABOUT THE AUTHOR

GEORGE GUIDA is the author of eight books, including *The Peasant and the Pen: Men, Enterprise and the Recovery of Culture in Italian American Narrative*. While publishing in Italian American studies since the 1990s, he has served as both President of the Italian American Studies Association (IASA) and as an incorporating officer of the Italian American Writers Association (IAWA).

Guida's critical writing has appeared in *Bookslut, The Columbia Journal of American Studies, The Encyclopedia of Ethnic American Literature, The Italian American Review, Italian Americana, The Journal of Italian Cinema and Media Studies, The Journal of Popular Culture, MELUS, The Paterson Literary Review, PMLA, Rain Taxi,* and *Voices in Italian Americana*.

He teaches English and creative writing at New York City College of Technology (CUNY) and Walden University, and co-edits *2 Bridges Review*.

SAGGISTICA

Taking its name from the Italian—which means essays, essay writing, or non-fiction—*Saggisitca* is a referred book series dedicated to the study of all topics and cultural productions that fall under what we might consider that larger umbrella of all things Italian and Italian/American.

Vito Zagarrio
  The "Un-Happy Ending": Re-viewing The Cinema of Frank Capra. 2011. ISBN 978-1-59954-005-4. Volume 1.
Paolo A. Giordano, Editor
  The Hyphenate Writer and The Legacy of Exile. 2010. ISBN 978-1-59954-007-8. Volume 2.
Dennis Barone
  America / Trattabili. 2011. ISBN 978-1-59954-018-4. Volume 3.
Fred L. Gardaphè
  The Art of Reading Italian Americana. 2011. ISBN 978-1-59954-019-1. Volume 4.
Anthony Julian Tamburri
  Re-viewing Italian Americana: Generalities and Specificities on Cinema. 2011. ISBN 978-1-59954-020-7. Volume 5.
Sheryl Lynn Postman
  An Italian Writer's Journey through American Realities: Giose Rimanelli's English Novels. "The most tormented decade of America: the 60s" ISBN 978-1-59954-034-4. Volume 6.
Luigi Fontanella
  Migrating Words: Italian Writers in the United States. 2012. ISBN 978-1-59954-041-2. Volume 7.
Peter Covino & Dennis Barone, Editors
  Essays on Italian American Literature and Culture. 2012. ISBN 978-1-59954-035-1. Volume 8.
Gianfranco Viesti
  Italy at the Crossroads. 2012. ISBN 978-1-59954-071-9. Volume 9.
Peter Carravetta, Editor
  Discourse Boundary Creation (LOGOS TOPOS POIESIS): A Festschrift in Honor of Paolo Valesio. ISBN 978-1-59954-036-8. Volume 10.
Antonio Vitti and Anthony Julian Tamburri, Editors
  Europe, Italy, and the Mediterranean. ISBN 978-1-59954-073-3. Volume 11.
Vincenzo Scotti
  Pax Mafiosa or War: Twenty Years after the Palermo Massacres. 2012. ISBN 978-1-59954-074-0. Volume 12.

Anthony Julian Tamburri, Editor
  Meditations on Identity. Meditazioni su identità. ISBN 978-1-59954-082-5. Volume 13.
Peter Carravetta, Editor
  Theater of the Mind, Stage of History. A Festschrift in Honor of Mario Mignone. ISBN 978-1-59954-083-2. Volume 14.
Lorenzo Del Boca
  Italy's Lies. Debunking History's Lies So That Italy Might Become A "Normal Country". ISBN 978-1-59954-084-9. Volume 15.

www.ingramcontent.com/pod-product-compliance
Lightning Source LLC
Chambersburg PA
CBHW022128080426
42734CB00006B/275